A work book of group-analytic interventions

Trainee therapists in groups often have to embark on an apprenticeship in which they learn by being an observer in a group or work almost immediately as a co-therapist. This is in many ways an excellent way of learning, but it is often difficult for the learner to go into his or her early groups with a full appreciation of the nature of intervention. This work book, written by senior and very experienced practitioners, gives the trainee a practical insight into the ways in which experienced group analysts may tackle difficult situations facing a group therapist.

Eight situations drawn from real psychotherapy groups are presented in detail to allow readers to exercise their own skills in taking decisions and making judgements about appropriate interventions. Each situation is then analysed in depth by one of the authors, and the thinking behind group psychotherapists' interventions is set out and commented on.

A Work Book of Group-Analytic Interventions gives the trainee a wide and informed appreciation of different situations arising in groups and appropriate ways of handling them, providing an excellent base from which to start to practise. The book will be invaluable to all students and teachers of group analysis as well as psychotherapists, counsellors, social workers, clinical psychologists and psychiatrists.

David Kennard is Consultant Clinical Psychologist at The Retreat in York, **Jeff Roberts** is Consultant Psychotherapist at the Royal London Hospital, and **David A. Winter** is District Clinical Psychologist for the Barnet Healthcare Trust.

With contributions from **Yiannis Arzoumanides**, group therapist and counsellor in private practice, and **Malcolm Pines**, the Group-Analytic Practice, London.

The International Library of Group Psychotherapy and Group Process

General Editor

Dr Malcolm Pines
Institute of Group Analysis, London, and formerly of the Tavistock Clinic, London.

The International Library of Group Psychotherapy and Group Process is published in association with the Institute of Group Analysis (London) and is devoted to the systematic study and exploration of group psychotherapy.

A work book of group-analytic interventions

David Kennard,
Jeff Roberts
and David A. Winter,
with contributions from
Yiannis Arzoumanides
and Malcolm Pines

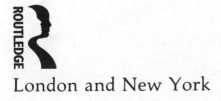

London and New York

First published in 1993
by Routledge
11 New Fetter Lane, London EC4P 4EE

Simultaneously published in the USA and Canada
by Routledge
29 West 35th Street, New York, NY 10001   212-244-3336   *orders* 1·800 634-7064

Typeset in Palatino by Witwell Ltd, Southport
Printed and bound in Great Britain by Clays Ltd, St. Ives PLC

British Library Cataloguing in Publication Data
A catalogue record for this book is available from the British Library.

Library of Congress Cataloging in Publication Data
A Work book of group-analytic interventions/David Kennard, Jeff Roberts, and David Winter, with contributions from Yiannis Arzoumanides and Malcolm Pines.
    p. cm. — (International library of group psychotherapy and group process)
Includes bibliographical references and index.
    1. Group psychoanalysis. 2. Group psychotherapy. I. Kennard, David, 1923- . II. Roberts, Jeff, 1944- . III. Winter, David A., 1950- . IV. Series.
[DNLM: 1. Psychoanalytic Therapy. 2. Psychotherapy, Group. WM 430 W926 1993]
RC510.W67 1993
616.89'17—dc20
DNLM/DLC
for Library of Congress   92-48526
                                                                             CIP

ISBN 0-415-08783-X
      0-415-08784-8 (pbk)

Contents

Figures and tables

FIGURES

TABLES

The authors and contributors

THE AUTHORS

David Kennard is a consultant clinical psychologist at The Retreat psychiatric hospital, York, and director of the Tuke Centre for Psychotherapy and Counselling, also in York. He is the author of *An Introduction to Therapeutic Communities* (Routledge, 1983) and editor of the journal *Therapeutic Communities*. He is a member of the Institute of Group Analysis.

Jeff Roberts is a consultant psychotherapist at the London Hospital who supervises doctors in training and has a large group-analytic practice. He is a member of the Institute of Group Analysis and has published several papers in the fields of therapeutic communities and group analysis. He co-edited with Malcolm Pines and contributed substantially to *The Practice of Group Analysis* published by Routledge in 1991.

David A. Winter is a District Clinical Psychologist for Barnet Healthcare NHS Trust, a Visiting Professor at the University of Hertfordshire and a member of the Group-Analytic Society. He has co-authored *Personal Styles in Neurosis*, published by Routledge & Kegan Paul in 1981, and is author of *Personal Construct Psychology in Clinical Practice*, published by Routledge in 1992, and of numerous papers in this area.

THE CONTRIBUTORS

Yiannis Arzoumanides is a psychologist and group psychotherapist trained at the London Centre for Psychotherapy. He has an MA in therapy and counselling from Antioch University. He currently works privately as a group therapist and counsellor, and is a member of the Group-Analytic Society (London). He teaches psychology and counselling in London and also conducts groups and workshops in Athens and London.

Malcolm Pines is a group analyst and psychoanalyst and currently a member of the Group-Analytic Practice where he now works full time having retired from the National Health Service. Prior to retirement he had held posts at both the Maudsley Hospital and the Tavistock Clinic. He has written numerous papers on group-analytic psychotherapy and with Earl Hopper founded the International Library of Group Psychotherapy and Group Process of which he is now the sole editor. He edited with Jeff Roberts *The Practice of Group Analysis* published by Routledge.

Acknowledgements

We would like to thank all those members of the Institute of Group Analysis who invested time, skill and effort in completing the Group Situations Questionnaire. The richness and variety of their responses were the stimuli which prompted us to produce this work book. Thanks are due to Linda Anderson, Harold Behr, Raymond Blake, Brian Boswood, Dennis Brown, Stephen Cogill, Vivienne Cohen, Elizabeth Foulkes, Keith Hyde, Nancy McKenzie, Jason Maratos, Bruce Marshall, George Renton, Kamran Saedi, Sheila Millard, Wyn Bramley, Gill Barratt, Eileen Berry, Raymond Blake, Janet Boakes, Bryan Boswood, Peter Bott, Jenny Duckham, Barbara Elliott, Sheila Ernst, Liza Glenn, Patricia Hughes, Michael Kelly, Terry Lear, Patrick de Maré, Angela Molnos, Gill Nathan, Pam Page, Herta Reik, Cynthia Rogers, Michael Sevitt, Una Stephenson, Paul Sepping, Beaumont Stevenson, Pauline Stevenson, Harry Tough, Hymie Wyse, Andrew Powell, Dick Blackwell and Jim Christie.

The work book is one of the products of a research project conducted by members of the Institute of Group Analysis and Group-Analytic Society Joint Research Committee. Various members of the committee have contributed substantially to the project over the past ten years. In addition to the authors, these have included Beaumont Stevenson, Tom Caine, Caroline Garland and Barbara Dick. Finally a special mention for John Cleaver, whose hard work on the project has included the transcribing of written responses of variable legibility to word-processor documents.

Introduction

This book is intended to provide the reader with a practical insight into the group-analytic method of group psychotherapy. The main body of the book contains a series of real-life situations from psychotherapy groups, each of which is followed by a range of possible interventions suggested by practising group analysts and a commentary by the authors on the nature of these interventions.

The material on which the book is based is drawn from a study by the Joint Research Committee of the Institute of Group Analysis and the Group-Analytic Society (London). In this study over thirty members of the Institute of Group Analysis responded to a questionnaire containing vignettes of situations occurring in psychotherapy groups which called for a response from the conductor. The respondents were asked to say what they would say or do in response to these situations. The purpose of the study was to explore the types of intervention that most characterise the practice of group analysis.

In carrying out this study (the detailed results of which are being prepared for publication in professional journals) it became apparent that the material we had collected represented a unique source of information about the way group analysts approach their work. Apart from videoing or sitting in on a large number of groups by different therapists – possible in principle, but constrained in practice by time, expense and ethical considerations – here is the most direct access to the thinking and personal styles of a large number of experienced group analysts.

Whilst acknowledging that responses to a questionnaire are not identical to what conductors would actually say in their groups, there can be little doubt that the variety and pungency of the suggested interventions reflect something of the individuality of their creators. Reading them is a powerful experience, enabling the reader to compare the interventions he or she might make with those of a large cross-section of experienced group therapists. The effect is illuminating, challenging and thought provoking. If we, the researchers, feel that way, surely others might value the same opportunity. Hence the idea of the work book was born.

In Chapter 1 Jeff Roberts investigates the nature of intervention and ways in which therapists attempt to intervene in the processes of their groups and their patients or clients in a helpful manner which is enabling rather than interfering. In the next chapter eight group situations are presented for readers to exercise their own intervention skills.

In the following eight chapters each of the situations is analysed in some depth by one of the authors of the book and selected interventions elicited from members of the Institute of Group Analysis in response to these situations are set out and commented on by the author.

In Chapter 11 Jeff Roberts looks further at the art of conducting groups and developing a therapeutic environment. In Chapter 12 Malcolm Pines gives his personal views on the nature of interpretation in psychotherapy. In this chapter a broader definition of interpretation is used than elsewhere in the book. This is followed by a concluding chapter which brings together some of the core features of the interventions presented in this book, and links them with the intervention categories described in Chapter 1. At the end of the book a short appendix outlines historically important contributions to the theory of group process and group therapy.

Our book is fundamentally a practical text so that no attempt at exhaustively reviewing the literature has been made. Group analysis has not yet gained a significant following in the United States so that only the seminal literature from this source is quoted. We hope in the future to see similar work books from the States and other countries which might illustrate other approaches to using the group as a therapeutic tool.

NOTES

The words client and patient are used more or less interchangeably, and the possible conflicts about the meaning of these words and the medicalisation of the psychotherapy patient' are not addressed.

For the readers' convenience and to facilitate commentary on and teaching from this book the therapist responses to the group situations are numbered consecutively from 1 upwards in chapters 3–10. (M) and (F) preceding conductor interventions indicate male and female conductors.

Chapter 1

Interventions

Jeff Roberts

This book is about interventions. In this chapter the meaning and implications of making an intervention are discussed. In the very broadest sense interventions are the means by which people interact with the world and each other to create or recreate a world to live in.

INTERVENTIONS IN THE WORLD

It is often helpful to enquire after the precise definitions of a word to understand the significance of its use. The *Oxford English Dictionary* (1971) provides both a full range of uses of a word and extensive annotation of its origins. The following are the meanings given by the *OED* for the word 'intervention'.

1. The action of intervening, 'stepping in', or interfering in any affair, to affect its course or issue. Now frequently applied to the interference of a state or government in the domestic affairs or foreign relations of another country.

2. Intermediate agency: the fact of coming in or being employed as an intermediary. [*Which may be*: a) of persons or b) of things.]

3. The fact of coming or being situated between in place, time, or order. *Which for instance may be*: an intervening thing, event or period of time.

Intervention is derived from Latin and means a coming between.[1] Interventions inevitably make up a substantial majority of human behaviour. They are made by those who desire and intend to influence some part of the world and the beings within it.[2]

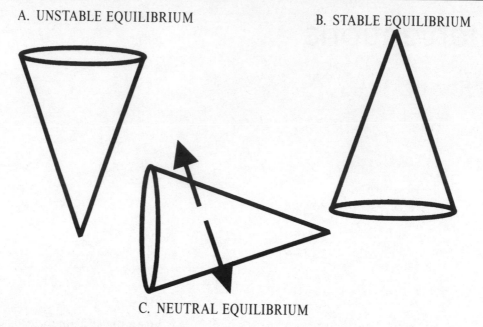

A. UNSTABLE EQUILIBRIUM

B. STABLE EQUILIBRIUM

C. NEUTRAL EQUILIBRIUM

Figure 1 Types of equilibrium

In the everyday physical world it is possible to observe processes[3] that are:

1. contributing to stable states (Figure 1B);

2. contributing to an unstable state (Figure 1A), likely to move off in another direction at any moment;

3. contributing to neutral equilibrium, in which movement is occurring but not leading to any significant change of state (Figure 1C);

4. contributing to a transition from one state to another (Figure 2).

INTERVENTION IN PSYCHOTHERAPY

People working in psychiatry and psychotherapy observe and participate in a wide range of psychological and mental processes and states. As in the simple physical example in Figure 1, the 'states' encountered may vary from extremely stable to very unstable. These states are perceived by various observers and interpreted according to the model of the mind which the observer is most comfortable with. Thus the behaviour of a member of a family who has attempted suicide may be variously interpreted as resulting from different kinds of process depending on the kind of model of the psychological causation one espouses. See Table 1.

Our patients/clients, their relatives, the police, the courts and we may deem some of

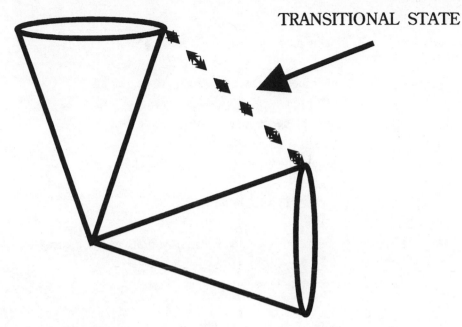

TRANSITIONAL STATE

Figure 2 A transitional state

Table 1 Models of psychological causation

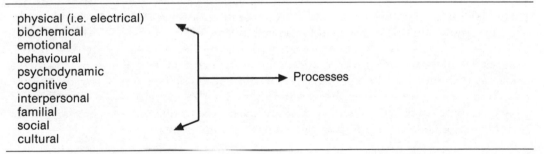

physical (i.e. electrical)
biochemical
emotional
behavioural
psychodynamic
cognitive
interpersonal
familial
social
cultural

Processes

these states or processes to be 'unhealthy' and worthy of changing. Practitioners who aim to treat people with various kinds of psychological disorder have devised a range of interventions, through which they intend to cause the current state or process to move in a positive direction.

Table 2 shows an attempt to outline the thinking that is likely to precede an intervention.

The medium of the psychotherapist's intervention is usually language. There are many different psychotherapies, and in each psychotherapy its practitioners aim to

Table 2 Deciding to intervene

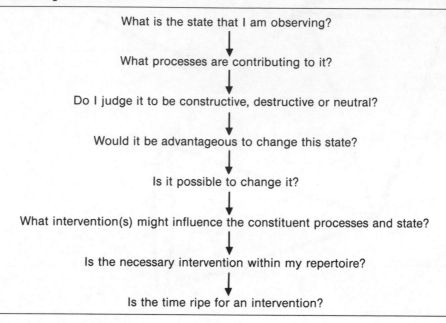

What is the state that I am observing?

↓

What processes are contributing to it?

↓

Do I judge it to be constructive, destructive or neutral?

↓

Would it be advantageous to change this state?

↓

Is it possible to change it?

↓

What intervention(s) might influence the constituent processes and state?

↓

Is the necessary intervention within my repertoire?

↓

Is the time ripe for an intervention?

apply various models of understanding of inter- and intrapersonal processes to secure a 'desired change' for individuals, couples, families or members of a stranger group. In each variety of therapy the underlying theory is variably precise and leads to a particular range of interventions. One example of an intervention in psychotherapy is the 'interpretation'. The basic intention behind an interpretation is to bring to the attention of one's patient/client aspects of his or her mental content that were previously unconscious. Interpretation is a central component of the psychoanalytic process and indeed is the core activity of the psychoanalyst (see Chapter 12). It is equally a core component of the various therapies that have been developed from a psychoanalytic base. The psychoanalytically orientated or dynamic psychotherapies can be included under this heading as can, in part, group analysis.

INTERVENTIONS IN GROUP ANALYSIS

It is important to bear in mind that a crucial intervention in psychotherapy is the actual decision to offer psychotherapy. A second significant intervention is the decision about what type of psychotherapy to recommend. Thus referral for group psychotherapy is an intervention in its own right as is also acceptance into a group. This will be discussed further from the point of view of the construction and care of an ongoing therapy group in Chapter 11. In this section, however, the types of intervention that a conductor may make during a group session are considered. This is the major focus of the book. In Chapter 2, eight group situations are presented. These situations are typical of some of the uncomfortable moments that a group therapist might experience. The reader is invited to generate the response he or she might have made in such a situation and compare these in succeeding chapters with responses made by experienced group analysts.

In the succeeding chapters the authors of this book, who have collaborated on a research project aimed at studying conductor interventions (Kennard *et al.*, 1990), analyse the situations and comment on the various interventions made by the trained group therapists. If the reader refers to these chapters, *after having made his or her interventions*, he or she will have an opportunity to give consideration in depth to these interventions and the thinking and feeling behind them, through comparing them with the range of proposed interventions.

To study the style of interventions of our conductors (in the research project), a classification of interventions was developed from studying initial responses to our group vignettes. This classification is still being evolved and may be compared to systems developed by other workers in the field (DiLoreto, 1971; Lieberman *et al.*, 1973; Wile, 1973; Nichols and Taylor, 1975). Along the way experience has shown that certain types of intervention, common in other methods of therapy, have less relevance to group analysis. These are, for instance, self-disclosure and modelling. These types of intervention have been retained in the system of classification, but are only occasionally regarded as the main feature of an intervention by group-analytic conductors.

A conceptual framework for the development of the new classification was a helpful analysis of the components of an ongoing therapy group made by Patrick de Maré (1972), who proposed that a group can be understood as comprising:

1. structure;

2. process;

3. content.

A not unnatural expectation of a group conductor would be that his or her interventions would aim to: a) maintain the structure of the group, b) facilitate the process and c) clarify the latent content of the statements and interactions in the group. It is possible to classify many if not all conductor interventions helped by this framework. Table 3 shows the system of classification which was originally proposed and Table 4 gives brief definitions of intervention types.

As well as the type of intervention, the research project was also concerned with the element of the group addressed by the intervention. Each intervention is likely to concern any of the following or any combination of them and their interrelationships:

- one or more individual members;
- the group as a whole;
- parts of the group, e.g. pairs, threesomes, all the women, all the men;
- the conductor.

Table 3 A classification of conductor interventions

1. Maintenance (structure)
2. Open facilitation (process)
3. Guided facilitation (process)
4. Interpretation (content)
5. No immediate response
6. Action
7. Self-disclosure
8. Modelling

Table 4 Definitions of intervention type

1. *Maintenance* interventions are those aimed at clarifying or re-affirming a relevant boundary. This may be a boundary of place, time, membership, task or permitted behaviour and may concern the boundaries of the group as a whole or of a particular member including the conductor.
2. *Open facilitation* is an intervention aimed at promoting the forward movement of the group process, but not based on any particular interpretative hypothesis on the part of the conductor and not referring to unconscious levels of awareness.
3. *Guided facilitation* includes all facilitating remarks that are not simply open-ended, but which indicate that the conductor has a hypothesis in mind, which is guiding his questioning, prompting and observations.
4. *Interpretation* involves verbal intervention by the conductor which makes manifest feelings or meanings which are latent in what the group as a whole or its individual members are saying.
5. *No immediate response* is a coding which acknowledges that during the course of an ongoing group, a significant part of the behaviour of the conductor will involve silent observation of his group. In response to the group situations, there will be occasions when the conductor does or says nothing in response to the situation, reserving the right to intervene later, depending on the further development of the situation.
6. *Action* refers to any kind of physical activity which the group conductor might engage in inside the group, which involves leaving his/her chair or touching another group member.
7. *Self-disclosure* is any declaration by the therapist about the content of his own inner world, or his outer world, which does not fit in any other category of intervention.
8. *Modelling* is any activity on the part of the conductor which contains an implicit intention that it should be identified with and become part of the repertoire of behaviour of the group or its members from whom it was previously absent. This would include coping adequately with distressing events, or uncomfortable social situations and also the modelling of an analytic, enquiring and concerned attitude.

The researchers' original intention was the characterisation of conductors or cohorts of conductors from particular schools of therapy. However, the idea of classifying interventions and attempting to identify an intervention and the intention behind its use is also a potentially valuable idea for those who are practising or learning to practise as therapists. Some use of this tool has also been made in the commentaries on the interventions of our team of group therapists in Chapters 3–10.

THE PSYCHOTHERAPIST'S THERAPEUTIC IDENTITY

The therapist's mode of intervening in his or her groups will be subject to many influences. One of these will be his or her personality structure, which is partly constitutionally determined but also very much influenced by life experiences. The more rigorous psychotherapy training schemes undoubtedly aim to access many areas of the individual's inner world and its structure to produce a more or less conforming graduate, whose personality and outlook will have been significantly modified or developed by the training experience. None the less many aspects of the therapist's personality and personal style will have remained relatively constant despite the influence of his or her therapy and training.[4]

The following are factors that are likely on a day to day basis to influence the interventions a therapist makes in his or her groups.

Constitutional (hereditary) characterological and temperamental traits. Thus, some psychotherapists seem to be impatient and unable to move at the pace of their client.

Life history. Inevitably each person follows his or her own unique pathway through life. Their expectation of what is normal and bearable will have been conditioned by this. The range of empathy possible for any given therapist will depend partly on life experience and it is not uncommon for therapists to take a special interest in those who appear to have trodden a similar pathway to themselves.

Major belief systems (religious or political).[5] Socialism, Christianity and Judaism are powerful belief systems which some people place high in their hierarchy of motivational influences. These are likely to influence therapeutic priorities. Sometimes, for instance, inexperienced feminist or anti-racist therapists may give 'therapeutic' attention to chauvinistic or racist content in their client's talk, rather than attending to the psychopathology which is causing him or her discomfort.

Current life events. The individual therapist is in the midst of his or her own life. Inevitably he or she will at times be disabled, distracted or overexcited by these events. A therapist whose own marriage is in difficulties may be over-empathic in relation to the marital problems of a patient.

Personal therapeutic experience (which may be past or ongoing). The success or otherwise of personal therapy will undoubtedly contribute to the comfort with which an individual practises, and influence his or her range of effectiveness and competence to a considerable extent. It is also commonly found that the style of a therapist has been influenced to a significant extent by the style of his or her own analyst or therapist.

Past and current supervisory experience. Supervisors have a similar influence to therapists. A good supervisor will have stretched his or her pupil and explored many areas of vulnerability, omnipotence and blindness. He or she will have also put forward a particular way of doing things and no doubt a clear-cut theoretical allegiance. Moreover, supervisors will have their own blind spots and maybe areas of hyper-acuity.

Training and thereby theoretical allegiance. Most therapists ally themselves to a school of therapy and will intervene according to theories arising from their allegiance. Traditional Freudians will tend to find oedipal conflicts where a Kleinian may perceive an ambivalent relationship with mother's breasts.

Into this complex system there arrives input from the group and from it comes output to the group.

LEARNING TO INTERVENE

Most therapists and counsellors have experienced themselves as having an intuitive desire to intervene helpfully in the psychological processes of others together with some natural skill in doing so. Gradually these people hone their skills in making such interventions. Usually these skills involve verbal interaction although they may also include other means of communication such as through music, art, dance and movement or through direct bodily contact. Eventually a counsellor or therapist may decide to train with one of the recognised psychotherapeutic institutes. The more sound teaching organisations will offer their carefully selected candidates a combination of theoretical seminars and supervised practice and, in the case of the psycho-analytic and humanistic institutes, have a system by which the candidate has a prolonged and intensive therapy of the type he or she intends to practise.

Emerging from such a training, the graduate will have a more or less clear understanding of the interventions from within his or her method that have major therapeutic effect. This will probably have at least three sources. The first will be implicit in the theories underpinning the method he or she has been trained to carry out and may be supported by evaluative research studies. The second will be derived from the therapist's conscious and unconscious appreciation of helpful interventions made by his or her therapist.[6] The third will be a partly unconscious and intuitive awareness of the type of verbal and non-verbal behaviours that lead to apparently good outcomes in his or her encounters with patients/clients. These antecedents of intervention may at times pull in different directions, setting up uncomfortable conflicts in the therapist. Resolving these conflicts will represent important steps in the maturation of a therapist. It will therefore take some years of post-qualification experience and further learning before a therapist has fully matured into his or her method.

This book intends to add a further learning tool to those available in group therapy training. It gives a method of exploring interventions in group therapy in imagination and adds the powerful experience of being able to compare the intervention that the reader might make with a series of interventions made by practising group analysts. It is important to remember, however, that, while this book focuses on therapist interventions, in a group-analytic group the interventions may come from others in the group and the most powerful intervention of the therapist may be *no immediate response*.

NOTES

1 Inter: meaning in Latin is, *between*.
  Venire: meaning in Latin is, *to come*.
2 This is interesting in itself since we find that some people are far more ready to intervene in world processes than others. Degrees of interventionism from *laissez-faire* through to intrusive interference can be recognised. Whatever type of intervener a person is, however, it is important psychologically and in other ways (such as legally) to accept responsibility for one's intervention or lack of it. In psychotherapy it is not uncommon to find individuals who avoid intervention at all costs, with the hope that they will thus avoid responsibility for real or fantasised damage resulting from the intervention.
3 A process may be defined as a series of actions or events.
4 These might include severe and masked global psychopathology, lacunae of severe disturbance and highly valued ideas which are more or less incompatible with central theoretical tenets of the chosen training. It is not uncommon for the gaining of a qualification to be more important than a dedicating of oneself to an intensive training experience.
5 Such systems are likely to be derived from a variety of influences and tend to be ordered in a hierarchy of importance as a result of both conscious and unconscious processes.
6 The recently qualified or indeed even experienced therapist may have identified with his own therapist's style of intervention in a non-critical way, so that in some ways both good and bad aspects of this most important of teachers' method may be acquired and can be modified later with some difficulty.

Chapter 2

Eight group situations

The eight group situations which are printed in this chapter will give you an opportunity to think what your own intervention(s) would be if you were the conductor of the group. These are all situations which have actually happened in groups. They all present possible turning or pivotal points in the life of the group and much depends in this sort of situation on how the crisis is resolved. A group could disintegrate, stagnate or become in other ways destructive to its members if dysfunctional solutions are adopted by the group. The conductor has an opportunity, through his or her intervention, to tip the balance of events towards favourable rather than unfavourable development.

Generally you should be able to imagine yourself in the situation described and have a feel for what is going on, for what has gone before and for what might happen in the future. When you have considered and perhaps written down your own intervention, it will be possible to refer to Chapters 3–10 to discover and study the interventions made by a number of experienced therapists, together with a commentary on these interventions from the authors of the book. This will give you a chance to evaluate your own intervention and think how it might have been different. You might find it a good exercise to repeat the responses after completing your reading of the book.

In the following pages each situation is presented at the top of the page, followed by three questions. The space below is for you to write your own initial ideas in response to these questions. After reading the rest of the book, you can see whether your understanding of each situation, and your likely response to it, has changed.

SITUATION 1

The first session – an apparent distraction

It is the first meeting of a new group. The six members begin by initiating a brief go-round giving their names but no other information. One member begins talking about therapy, and mentions the name of Carl Rogers. Another then produces an advertisement torn from a newspaper about a Ronald Laing workshop taking place locally in a week or so, and offers it round to the other members.

1. Write down your understanding of the situation, i.e. What's going on? How did things get to be like this?

2. What intervention, if any, would you make?

3. Finally write briefly your reasons for making this intervention.

SITUATION 2

Turn taking in the early sessions

In a new group the members have established a pattern of each member in turn taking a session to 'tell his tale of woe'. The others listen and advise and therapise. It is now the sixth session and the turn of (X). He begins.

1. Write down your understanding of the situation, i.e. What's going on? How did things get to be like this?

2. What intervention, if any, would you make?

3. Finally write briefly your reasons for making this intervention.

SITUATION 3

A potential drop-out

The group is two months old. In the first few weeks two members dropped out without any discussion about leaving. Another member, John, has now missed two sessions without sending a message. In these two sessions members expressed some concern about John's seeming to be depressed and socially isolated. At the next session John arrives a few minutes late. One member greets him cheerfully, 'Hello, John, nice to see you'. Following this the other members proceed to talk about negative attitudes of work colleagues towards psychotherapy and to discuss in a rather intellectual way why people get depressed. Nothing is said to John, who remains silent.

1. Write down your understanding of the situation, i.e. What's going on? How did things get to be like this?

2. What intervention, if any, would you make?

3. Finally write briefly your reasons for making this intervention.

SITUATION 4

A member seeks approval for concurrent individual therapy

This group has been meeting for a year. An attractive young woman (one of five siblings) has, after a difficult start in which she tended to be a monopoliser, apparently settled in and become a rather more integrated group member. You are nevertheless aware that she has intense and unresolved problems of rivalry with her mother in relation to her father. Today she announces, with coy hesitation, that she is sure the group is going to be very angry with her because she has, unbeknown either to them or to her female group therapist, been seeing a male psychotherapist on an individual basis for the past six months. The group respond warmly and supportively to her disclosure, commend her for her courage in making it and encourage her to continue to make use of both therapeutic modalities. She turns to you and asks prettily if you mind.

1. Write down your understanding of the situation, i.e. What's going on? How did things get to be like this?

2. What intervention, if any, would you make?

3. Finally write briefly your reasons for making this intervention.

SITUATION 5

An invitation to a Christmas party

It is the last session before the Christmas break in a group that has now been meeting for a year. The members have been unable, in spite of much hard work on your part, to accept their denial of anxiety over the impending separation – in fact they all appear extremely cheerful. On this occasion one member brings in unexpectedly a basket, full of home-made mince-pies, which smell delicious, and another member a bottle of wine and glasses for everyone, including the therapist.

1. Write down your understanding of the situation, i.e. What's going on? How did things get to be like this?

2. What intervention, if any, would you make?

3. Finally write briefly your reasons for making this intervention.

SITUATION 6

Threatened premature termination of therapy

A single woman in her thirties, who has been in the group for a year, announces that she is going to leave in four weeks' time – the notice period asked for in the initial guidelines given to members. Although she has gained in confidence during the year, the timing seems premature as there are areas of difficulty which have only begun to be explored in the group – in particular her difficulty in dealing with her own and others' aggressive feelings in the group. When asked by other members to talk about her reasons for leaving, her answers are vague – she does not feel she can get what she wants in this particular group. When pressed further she says she does not really understand it herself. It is now the last of the four sessions of the notice period and it is not clear whether she still intends to leave or has changed her mind.

1. Write down your understanding of the situation, i.e. What's going on? How did things get to be like this?
2. What intervention, if any, would you make?
3. Finally write briefly your reasons for making this intervention.

SITUATION 7

Disillusionment with therapy

This group has been meeting for over two years and their early idealisations of the group and its conductor have been replaced by varying styles and degrees of disillusionment. Today the group chorus is concerned with the uselessness of psychotherapy. You do not respond and they repeat the theme more loudly until one by one they fall silent. The silence has lasted for fourteen minutes and there are three minutes to go before the end of the group.

1. Write down your understanding of the situation, i.e. What's going on? How did things get to be like this?

2. What intervention, if any, would you make?

3. Finally write briefly your reasons for making this intervention.

SITUATION 8

A threat of physical violence

A borderline patient has been in an established group for 18 months. She seems unable to take in any group support and her moods change quite quickly. In this session four of the six members are present. The patient is unable to get her feelings out about the therapist. Near the end of the group she erupts in violence and, producing a razor blade, she threatens to 'carve you up'. Two members flee in panic.

1. Write down your understanding of the situation, i.e. What's going on? How did things get to be like this?

2. What intervention, if any, would you make?

3. Finally write briefly your reasons for making this intervention.

Chapter 3

The first session – an apparent distraction

David Kennard

SITUATION 1

It is the first meeting of a new group. The six members begin by initiating a brief go-round giving their names but no other information. One member begins talking about therapy, and mentions the name of Carl Rogers. Another then produces an advertisement torn from a newspaper about a Ronald Laing workshop taking place locally in a week or so, and offers it round to the other members.

THE THERAPIST'S TASK AND PROBLEMS

The therapist in this situation has an overriding task, to help the group get started, moving approximately in the direction he or she would like it to go. There is much involved here potentially: listening, modelling, promoting safety, exploring defences, demonstrating group processes at work.

Let us take listening first, since that is what the therapist is doing. We can infer that he or she has taken a back seat so far, waiting to see what happens, having set the group up. What is he or she listening to? On the surface, members introducing themselves, then veering away from the group to talk about other therapists and other groups. This is unlikely to be a coincidence. Indeed from a group-analytic point of view the apparent topic, whatever it is, will always have an unconscious resonance with a concern that some or all members are experiencing within the group. So the listening is an active listening, scanning the content of the conversation for psychological parallels with the group.

In this case the parallel is not hard to find. They are talking about therapy and therapists, exchanging information about this new kind of venture they have all just embarked on. What parallels does this have with the present situation? Might they be in the underlying questions the group members are asking? 'What kinds of therapy are there? What kinds of therapists are there?' translates as 'What kind of therapy and therapist do we have? If we know more about these things will we be better able to cope with what is going to happen here?'

So one theme is uncertainty about what the group has in store. That theme probably is shared by all the group members. Whatever preparation they may have had, the actual future of this group is still a mystery to everyone, including the therapist.

The therapist will also notice the behaviour of individuals. Two have taken the lead, and are offering themselves to the others as guides or sources of knowledge. What guesses can we make to understand what this means for the individuals concerned, who, like all the members, are facing a group of strangers for the first time? A desire to demonstrate to the others their knowledge, helpfulness or enthusiasm? Wanting to impress the therapist with the same? Wanting to displace the therapist? An anxiety that the group may somehow fall apart in the silence? These and other interpretations are possible, but it would be a rash therapist who would venture a judgement without further evidence. The therapist also notices the behaviour of the other members – do they respond with interest or keep to themselves? We are not told, but must assume that reactions range along this continuum.

The therapist notices the behaviour of individuals but does little with this information at present, partly because the information is still very incomplete, but more importantly because the task which faces the therapist at present would not be facilitated by exploring the feelings or motives of individual members.

As pointed out above, the paramount task right now is to help the group get started. This is its fledgling flight and at this stage the following short-term criteria apply to everything the therapist is considering saying or doing. In other words the therapist will need to ask him or herself the question: is what I am going to say (or have just said) likely to help towards the following goals in this session?

First goal

By the end of the session all members should feel able to come back the following week. No one should have felt so exposed, so ignored, so frightened, so disillusioned that they want to give up on the group there and then. To this end the therapist must stay alert for how each member of the group might be feeling, intervening if he or she senses that someone may be jeopardising their own or someone else's future in the group, and refraining from intervening in a way that might lead to an intolerable increase in anxiety for one or more members.

Second goal

The group needs to feel safe at the same time as promising something for the future. There is balance here. Too much safety and the question may arise in members' minds:

what's the point of coming? Too strong an intimation of underlying wishes or fears and members may withdraw quickly to a safe distance, emotionally if not physically.

When in doubt about the balance the therapist should give priority to the needs of the group as a whole and err on the side of safety. Most members will appreciate it if they see that the therapist does not intend to let anyone turn themselves into a sacrificial offering on the first day nor do they intend to use their superior position and knowledge to criticise, humiliate or ridicule anyone.

Yet the group also needs to feel that here there is promise of help and relief, that this is something different from a social club, an evening with friends – even close ones – a seminar or discussion group. The therapist needs to intervene in ways that show he or she understands what is going on and what people may be feeling, without doing this in a way that makes anyone feel too exposed or undermined. The message has to be: here is potential for change, here too are safe boundaries.

Third goal

The therapist has an opportunity to begin modelling the kind of behaviour he or she hopes will become the norm for the group. Self-disclosure about here-and-now thoughts or feelings of a not too revealing kind may help, or direct but non-threatening comments or questions to individuals, e.g. 'I'm glad you said that, I was feeling something similar'. These kinds of interventions help not only to set the tone for the group, but also indirectly indicate what will not happen. They can indicate that the group will not be a forum for intellectual discussion about general issues nor a place where conventional rules of social etiquette prevail, but neither will it be a hot-house of confrontation and forced personal growth. Obviously the group will have to work on developing its norms for a period of weeks or months, but the therapist can begin to set the tone from the outset.

Another important task the therapist has at this stage is to be aware of and cope with his or her own feelings about the group and his or her role in it. He or she is likely to be feeling a number of things, many of which cannot – or should not – be shared with the group, at least at this early stage. The therapist is likely to have anxieties and uncertainties, such as 'How will they get on together? Will they all keep coming? Will I say too much? Too little?' Perhaps there are group therapists who face the first session of a new group with equanimity, but this is rare and would raise questions about the therapist's sensitivity. It can be an exhilarating experience too, the culmination of months of preparation and interviewing. Both the painful and pleasant feelings of the therapist need to be kept in awareness but, except where they serve a positive purpose for the group, out of interventions at this stage. The group does not want to be burdened with the therapist's doubts about his or her competence or judgement at this point.

One interpretation of the present group situation that may be made (internally) by an anxious or insecure therapist is that it is a reflection of the therapist's own inadequacy in contrast to other more famous therapists. Here the therapist's difficult task is to tolerate and stand back from the feeling of inadequacy in order to separate out two components: 1) the information it provides about the unconscious anxiety or question being posed by individuals within and possibly on behalf of the group: will you look after us as well as these other therapists could? 2) the therapist's own personal doubts about his or her competence. In other words the therapist must try to cope with feeling undermined and possible feelings of anger or resentment towards individual members and hold on to these feelings until he or she has had a chance to reflect on them and determine their sources. If this can be done during the group an appropriate and helpful response might be to comment on the unconscious question being posed.

One of the paradoxes and frustrations of first sessions is that a great deal of meaning may be revealed or implied in the way individuals deal with this new and strange situation, yet the therapist cannot comment too directly to individuals on this without jeopardising the sense of safety in the group.

It is also a fact that relative to any group therapist's general experience, experience of first sessions is bound to be limited – the more so the more long term are the groups he or she runs.

SELECTED INTERVENTIONS

Having commented on the group situation presented, and on the situation of first sessions generally, let us look at how a number of group therapists have said they would deal with this particular moment.

(F) 'I think people are probably feeling quite anxious about the sort of group this is going to be, and what is going to happen here.' (1)

The therapist focuses on making explicit the parallel connection between the topic and the member's underlying concern about the immediate situation. It is a simple, straightforward interpretation at the group level of what is, at that moment, unconscious or at least unspoken in the group.

(F) No comment – allow group to proceed. (2)

Therapist notes – *A comment could be too controlling. Various challenges to the conductor can allow members to begin expressing their views.*

The therapist perceives what is happening in terms of the challenge to the therapist by some members, and decides to avoid giving any direct response to this. This is consistent with my comments earlier about the need for the group to feel safe, including safe from criticism by the therapist, which at this early stage could appear punitive. Note that saying nothing is an active choice by the therapist, based on a perception of the needs of the group at this time.

(M) 'I'm wondering if it's easier to talk about the therapy group you might have been in or the one you might go to, rather than the one you're in the middle of right now.' (3)

Therapist notes – *At this early stage I'm trying to be gentle and encouraging but also to model a bit of directness.*

As in the first intervention, the therapist comments on the parallel subject matter, but in this case restricts himself to commenting on the defence – that the group is avoiding something potentially difficult – rather than commenting directly, as the first therapist did, on the presence of anxiety. Such an intervention may be described as a guided facilitation, since the therapist is leading the members towards the interpretation that they are anxious about this group, but is leaving the recognition of this for the group to come to. As the therapist notes, this is a gentle approach, less challenging than the first intervention. He also notes that there is some deliberate modelling, for reasons similar to those discussed above: to indicate the kind of behaviour the therapist is hoping to foster in others, which confronts avoidance rather than going along with it.

(M) 'I would be silent but listen attentively and encouragingly.' (4)

Therapist notes – *A group needs its defences, especially at the beginning. The necessary early lesson is that everything you say is listened to with interest and, at this stage, without implied criticism.*

This needs little extra comment.

(F) Blank response awaiting further developments. (5)

Therapist notes – *I would see the group as anxious about themselves and the possibilities of this group therapy. Probably some member(s) will indicate that the group was important and recall the preparatory work I would have done with each member.*

It is interesting to see that therapists (as well as patients) can be quiet for different reasons. This therapist is concerned about the devaluing of the group, but is relying on the members to balance this by coming in with comments on the importance of the group and by recalling the preparatory work done. Trusting the group right from the start is an important part of the group therapist's role. In this situation the therapist might decide to intervene later on if the group continued to focus on external material.

(M) 'I get the impression that the group has got on a train but isn't too sure whether it is the right one. It is difficult to experience a journey before it has begun.' (6)

Therapist notes – *A type of typical start with group searching to find out what type of group it is plus natural tendency to look for life-savers in case of emergency.*

The therapist is referring to the group's parallel concern with the here-and-now through the metaphor of a train journey. The second sentence could be taken as reassurance – in effect, 'don't worry, it's always difficult at this stage' – or as a mild rebuke – in effect, 'you are in too much of a hurry'. This ambiguity, combined with the use of a metaphor so early in the group's life, marks the therapist out as the interpreter and guide of the group, and is likely to reinforce his position as a potentially disapproving authority figure in the group.

(F) 'Now that we are all here together, we hardly know how to begin, or what to expect might happen.' (7)

Therapist notes – *I would be trying to make a 'joining' statement which would be designed to address and contain the anxiety of this first meeting.*

The therapist is aware of the parallel between the content of the topic and its underlying meaning, but does not refer to this. Rather than link the defence with the anxiety (which can be done implicitly or explicitly – see first and third interventions above) only the anxiety is referred to. This may be puzzling to those members who are not conscious of their anxiety. For members who are aware of their anxiety it is an intervention which, despite the therapist's intention, may heighten anxiety by refer-ring to it so directly, and without the comforting sense that the therapist understands and can give meaning to what is happening. In this sense it is the opposite kind of intervention to the one immediately preceding it. The former conveyed the therapist's power to understand, this conveys the therapist's powerlessness to do so.

(F) 'It seems that people in this group are pretty keen to get help.' (8)

Therapist notes – *1) Go with the moment. Plenty of time later to talk (another session – in say two months' time) about not putting all their energy/interest in THIS group. 2) Stress the positive. 3) Don't stir up the resistance just yet.*

A skilfully low key and supportive way to make the parallel link: the out-there/in-here connection is made with deliberate avoidance of drawing attention to the existence of the defence–anxiety link. The therapist's reasoning is clear from the comments made. The aim here appears to be to get the group members to start talking about themselves without introducing them to ideas about the processes going on in the group, as most previous interventions have done. In a sense it is quite a controlling intervention with the therapist taking a concealed supervisory role over the group's development. In making it the therapist is treading on a tightrope, as its effect will depend on how it is heard: any impression of the therapist's tongue being in her cheek would destroy the intended effect, implying criticism and disdain, and arousing the resistance that the therapist is wanting to postpone to a later session.

(F) I would say something to the effect that we have all been looking forward to today's meeting – we are all new as a group etc. and how do we feel – what do we hope etc. (9)

Therapist notes – *I think one explanation of this behaviour may be a need to control and fill the strange situation with a tangible plan/programme. In a group new to each other I would want to be cautious yet be firm in my offering of a structuring of our own to hold that anxious feeling.*

The therapist here is responding not to the parallel content of the topic but to the function it performs in 'filling the void' of a strange situation. The intervention would be an open, non-directive facilitation, recognising the need for some structure and implicitly pushing to the sidelines the structure offered by the group members. With what effects? The group may feel reassured by the therapist's firmness but also that they have to follow the therapist's agenda. The therapist has not tried to avoid appearing authoritative or stirring up resistance, and has put her leadership style firmly centre stage.

(M) My initial immediate non-verbal response would be to look up, open my eyes wider, and invite discussion. For a first group I'd be delighted for such potentially rich material. To continue the discussion I might say something like 'Laing has stood up against the medical profession'. (10)

Therapist notes – *I would be expecting there to be several reasons for this talk:*

a) *interest, excitement and hope in a new group.*

b) *the anxiety about what would happen here.*

c) *the question of whether they'll get what they really need.*

d) *Fear of total commitment to this group. Fear of rejection.*

e) *Questions about me as a leader – my competence, my fame.*

f) *Confrontation with my authority, and anger at my 'knowing' and their need of me. I would not want group members to go to these meetings.*

This therapist has thought out most of the possibilities! His optimism is infectious and one feels that he will positively enjoy the group's resistance. It is perhaps worth noting that the therapist here is a doctor – so his comment about Laing may be seen as drawing attention to the parallel between the members' feelings of approval for Laing and their desire to stand up against their medical group therapist. He is also clear that he would not want group members to attend the workshop – presumably because this would be acting out their feelings towards the group or its therapist – although it is not clear how he would convey this to the group.

(M) 'I suppose everyone wonders and must be anxious about, what they are in for. . .and wonders what group psychotherapy is all about. . .you probably wonder if you will meet outside, and what then. . .' (11)

Therapist notes – *I would want to stimulate/support boundary making. . .and to avoid taking a position on Laing etc.*

Both the previous and this therapist have drawn attention to a hitherto unmentioned issue, which is the boundary between what happens in the group and potential meetings and shared activities outside the group. Any kind of analytic work requires this boundary to be strictly observed, as not to do so risks a defensive dilution of the group experience and an acting out of feelings rather than bringing them to the group. The need for this is not always apparent to group members in a new group, even if they have been told this prior to joining. If the therapist suspects that some members may be embarking on outside meetings it may be necessary to tell them not to. The group will probably be relieved at this as it affirms the therapist's commitment to the group and its status as somewhere different from ordinary social life.

Chapter 4

Turn taking in the early sessions

David A. Winter

SITUATION 2

In a new group the members have established a pattern of each member in turn taking a session to 'tell his tale of woe'. The others listen and advise and therapise. It is now the sixth session and the turn of (X). He begins.

THE THERAPIST'S TASK AND PROBLEMS

Discussing the culture promoted during group analysis, Foulkes (1975, p. 95) describes the kind of verbal communication fostered as a 'free-floating discussion'. For him, 'The keynote to the group-analytic situation is its flexibility and its spontaneity, and these two, from the very beginning, give it its specific character. The group meets and shapes itself into a circle. And that is all the formality there is. There is no set topic for discussion, no rules of procedure, no programme, no leader' (Foulkes and Anthony, 1957, p. 70).

The situation described in this particular group therefore presents the therapist with a paradox. Clearly it is not one in which discussion flows freely, without procedural rules. However, presumably it is the very flexibility and spontaneity characterising the group-analytic situation which has allowed this particular group to arrive at its turn-taking pattern. For the therapist to intervene in such a way as to interfere with this pattern would be for him or her to impose a rule of procedure on the group.

Despite this latter consideration, it may be that some therapists will consider turn taking to be so obstructive to the effective running of the group that it behoves them to break the pattern. Yalom (1985), for example, includes turn taking in his category of 'antitherapeutic group norms', and describes how it may force some members into premature self-disclosure or generate such anxiety that it causes them to terminate therapy. His recommended method of intervening in such cases is to make a comment directed towards the whole group, which describes the process which is operating and its possible deleterious effects on group members, as well as indicating that alternative patterns of interaction in the group are possible.

A further issue on which the therapist's intervention might focus is the possible reason which the group might have for adopting this particular pattern of interaction. The early sessions of a psychotherapy group are almost invariably anxiety provoking for members, who are likely to look in vain to the therapist to provide the security of structure and guidance on how to interact. The group in the example may have despaired of receiving directions from the therapist, and instead arrived at its own procedural rules. Furthermore, the particular rules which they have developed have allowed them to address another problem which they faced, namely how to ensure that each member has an equal share of precious group time. In so doing, they have been able to avoid, at least for the time being, difficult feelings of envy, for example of members who are monopolising the group. By drawing attention to such aspects of the turn-taking pattern, the therapist may be able not only to interrupt the pattern but to demonstrate to the group a central feature of the culture which he or she may hope will develop in the group: the focus on the analysis of members' feelings and ways of behaving in the group.

Although useful purposes may, therefore, be served by an intervention which focuses on the group's interaction pattern rather than on the content of members' 'tales of woe', there is a major factor which may make the therapist hesitate to intervene in this instance. This is that to do so would be rather hard on X, who is just beginning his tale, and on any other members who have yet to have their turn. If the therapist does choose to draw the group's attention to the examination of its own behaviour, and therefore away from the tale which X is starting to relate, he or she is at least likely to attempt to frame the intervention concerned in such a way as to minimise the extent to which it may be perceived as rejecting towards, or indeed overly protective of, X.

How did our sample of group analysts tackle this difficult problem?

SELECTED INTERVENTIONS

For several therapists, this was a situation in which they would think it best not to intervene if they had not succeeded in breaking the turn-taking pattern by the sixth session. Some of their reasons for not responding were as follows:

(F) I would not have allowed this group to develop in this fashion. (1)

(M) I think I would do what I'd done for the other five. (Why shouldn't X get his turn?) And I'd wonder why I thought in terms of 'telling their tale of woe'. If I thought they were wasting time, why have I waited five sessions to challenge? Or have they been saying something important about themselves to each other that I haven't understood? (2)

(F) I might say nothing unless I felt he or she would be damaged by the demand to speak up – this is unlikely since I hope my selection process would have assured me that there was enough ego strength to begin, at least! (3)

Therapist notes – *I would wish I had pointed out that 'turn taking' was not mandatory or desirable (necessarily) earlier in the life of the group.*

Other therapists, while also not making an immediate intervention, would comment on the group's interaction pattern when X had completed his tale, or at least paused. For example:

(F) Let him go on – let the group respond. Towards the end of this session say 'It seems to me that this group is falling into a pattern of one member/one session. How do people feel about that?' (4)

Therapist notes – *DON'T CUT ACROSS IT – FOLLOW THE GROUP – Then later help them to start THINKING.*

(F) (a) Non-verbal at the beginning – leave things be, but not participate with the group in their response to the patient.
(b) During the course of the session – I would use interventions to direct attention or enquiry back to other group members who advise or therapise or, better still, to what the group as a whole is doing.
(c) If (b) does not produce any change in the approach of the group, I would wait until the 'going around' was finished and then, towards the end of the session, I'd say – 'perhaps it will be interesting, even valuable, to see what develops now today's "agenda", so to speak, has been completed'. Any further attempts to establish an agenda would be responded to by me with a question such as 'Why did you suggest that?' or a statement 'Perhaps it feels safer to know what might develop next, as if it's important to control things' or 'You seem to be afraid it would be unfair to let things develop freely' and later 'Could that feel a little dangerous?' (5)

Therapist notes – *If it has gone on as far as five (presumably out of eight) persons, it could be experienced by the remaining three as a provocatively depriving act to initiate a different treatment for the rest of the group. Better to be less explicit, and even to allow the last two or three an opportunity to feel similarly treated – it's possible, of course, that one or two will not want the whole group's attention for so long at this stage. I certainly would not call a halt to today's 'star'. My response would depend on what I felt to be appropriate to the group at the time. I might even simply state 'It seems we still need to stick to an "agenda".'*

(F) I would not intervene – certainly I would not deny X his turn when all the others have had a turn. Afterwards I would probably ask the group 'Do you think that it's easier to listen to our stories than for us to talk to each other here?' (6)

Therapist notes – *At the seventh session I might start the group by saying: 'Now that we know so much about each other – I wonder how we can get to know each other here?'*

(M) I'd let him go on a while and then, at a pause, I would say, 'I'm interested in what you've been saying, X. It seems to me that we could go on taking turns in each session for the duration of the group. Could it be a way of dealing with everyone's wish to be the only patient? It's as though everyone is afraid of being greedy or neglected.' (7)

Therapist notes – *The anxiety needs to be confronted to enable a freer pattern of exchange to develop. I might use the image of them assuming the group is a finite cake provided by the therapist, rather than a pot of soup which everyone contributes to as well as eats from.*

The comments which these therapists make after X has been allowed his turn to tell his story for a while range from a very open facilitatory remark to one which is more directly interpretative. In each case, however, the intention is to lead the group towards examination of its interaction pattern. Other therapists would look for an opportunity presented by the content of X's story, or the group's reaction to it, to make an intervention of this nature. Examples of their responses are as follows:

(F) I would wait until one of the tales of woe clearly mirrored what was happening in the group, e.g. a frustration of going round in circles. Then make an interpretation such as 'I wonder whether it's a bit like that here, that somehow we have got into a pattern and no-one likes to break it.' (8)

Therapist notes – *I would want to be sure I was harnessing their frustration and not simply mine. Also to get them in a non-threatening way to begin to explore the notion of resistance.*

(M) Very tricky. I think if the defence seemed to be suiting the group I might let things run until everyone had had a turn. But if I sensed much dissatisfaction at how things were going I might say:

> Poor old Arthur Flinagan
> He grew whiskers on his chin again
> The wind came out and blew them in again
> Begin again
> Poor old A . . . (9)

Therapist notes – *The question is when is the time ripe to confront a defence and if it is time how to do so without seeming to attack the group and particularly X who is speaking. A slightly crazy slightly funny intervention feels best – provided X is neither Irish nor called Arthur nor unshaven.*

A primary concern for both these therapists is not to threaten the group unduly. The second response illustrates the fact that group analysts' interventions are by no means always explicit, erudite analyses of the behaviour of groups or their members, but instead are often much more obscure remarks which aim to nudge the group towards self-examination. While such remarks will need to be sufficiently intriguing to the group that members will wish to explore the puzzle which they may initially present, they will be of questionable value if perceived by the group as so 'crazy' that they lead to consideration of the therapist's sanity rather than of the group process, or the avoidance of this difficult issue by ignoring the remark. The reader may wish to judge whether this therapist would be likely to achieve his aim of facilitating exploration by the group of its interaction pattern, or whether a good deal of further work by him, perhaps including some clarification of his reasons for breaking into rhyme, might be required.

While none of the therapists in the above examples would make an immediate intervention, in many cases because of the effect that this might have on X, others would have interrupted X, but in a way which acknowledges that it is his 'turn'. For example:

(F) 'X is the last one in the group to talk about his problem. When you have heard it you may wonder what to do next. In order to take the next step you may perhaps look at what has happened in the group so far.' (10)

(M) 'I get the impression that maybe you feel it's "your turn" tonight.' (11)

Therapist notes – *which leaves it open for him to look at whether it's his turn for a treat or a chore – looking forward, or dreading? Which would I hope lead into the question of how the group came to start up this 'rota' for themselves.*

(M) (1) Turn to X. Ask him what he thinks his 'tale of woe' means – lead the group into talking about meaning instead of advice. (2) Reflect (aloud) on how the whole group has developed a pattern of 'advice'. What does it mean? (12)

Therapist notes – *Group interpretation to start with would be rejecting to X. Pattern described suggests conductor has been too inactive in imbuing group with therapeutic culture. Therefore conductor has to step in. First 'work with X' (shows the group how to 'work'), then with the group.*

These three therapists are therefore attempting to lead the group to examine its interaction pattern, or guide it towards a more therapeutic pattern, but without rejecting X. While in every case the intervention refers to X, and in the last two examples is directed towards him, it should be noted that it does not concern the content of his 'tale', since this would only be likely to imply support for, and to perpetuate, the turn taking and advice giving. In the second example, the therapist skilfully makes an intervention which demonstrates attention to X, and acknowledgement of his right to hold the floor, but which invites him to talk about the turn-taking pattern rather than to recount a tale. In the third, a significant component of the intervention is modelling by the therapist of a more productive style of interaction. Other therapists also indicate in their intervention the possibility of an interaction pattern which involves not 'therapising' and being 'therapised' but sharing of feelings engendered by members' tales. For example:

(F) I'd let X begin, but watch his material carefully – there must be something that 'meshes' with the stories others have told. Then I'd start reflecting, bring in group members who must identify/reciprocate similar feelings, e.g. 'X had this problem with his mother, but you are a mother of teenagers, Jane . . .' (only neater than that I hope) or 'you've also lost a partner, William . . .' (13)

Therapist notes – . . . *I have a 'picture' of stained glass work; sheets of single-coloured glass must be cut up and intermingled to make a far more interesting pattern – I may share this analogy with the group.*

(F) 'There is something happening in this group and I think we should stop and think about it. This week Liz is being the patient and everyone else the therapist. Last week Joe and so on. I wonder if we're all afraid of competing for attention, perhaps feelings would get so strong they could get out of hand, even violent. Maybe someone would get hurt, perhaps me.' I would also ask direct questions to members: 'I know that you had difficulty with your father, Tom, rather like Liz. How do you feel listening to her?' (14)

Therapist notes – *This pattern avoids confronting the individual's need of the therapist and 'kills off' therapist by letting rest of group therapise. Thus need, greed and frustration are avoided.*

While the therapists in the above examples, if choosing to intervene, all make some reference to X in their remarks, others appear less concerned about X's possible reaction to an intervention which seems largely to ignore him. They would have intervened thus:

(M) 'Each week we have one patient and six therapists. Why do you think this is?' (15)

Therapist notes – *I would definitely make a group response to a group resistance.*

(M) 'Oh dear. I wonder what is going to happen when you have all had your chance to tell us your story. Start all over again? Or will you expect me to sum up?' (16)

Therapist notes – *This pattern needs challenging, yet I am aware that early on a challenge might feel sarcastic or persecutory.*

(F) 'I have noticed over the weeks that you all seem to have silently agreed to stick to a certain pattern in the group where you equally share out the time and attention in the group. Any ideas about this?' (17)

Therapist notes – *I assume that the reason for the formation of this structure is in the service of defending against feelings of greed and insatiability. I would want to say something that might help them catch hold of these feelings more directly in conscious thought.*

(M) 'When you take your turn everyone is insisting on scrupulous equality of opportunity in the group, all for one – one for all. Is it true that words of individuals will occur according to timetable? How far is it true that any one member's experience is exclusive to him or her? You cling to individual experience yet join together to do so. Joining together must be carefully controlled for some reason.' (18)

Therapist notes – *The fear behind the behaviour may be that of losing identity.*

(M) 'Let's take a look at the process a moment. A pattern seems to have emerged – each one bringing the family album along in turn – I wonder whether the group is avoiding something by this. It seems that the group feels the only way to function is to take it in turns – perhaps people are worried about not getting a say otherwise.' (19)

Therapist notes – *To suggest there might be other ways of working.*

(M) 'I wonder if our recent "let's talk one-at-a-time roundabout" is a way of saying that it feels dangerous to compete for a place in the group at the moment without this extra safety net.' (20)

Therapist notes – *I would interpret it as a temporary phenomenon to focus on present feelings, rather than as a traditional pattern which the group has set up. This would keep it focused on the here and now.*

(F) 'Perhaps by being so helpful to each other and taking turns so politely you are demonstrating feelings about me as leader or "parent" in the group. It suggests to me that there may be some very anxious, maybe angry, feelings around about my leaving you to fend for yourselves.' (21)

Therapist notes – *The group is at a very early stage of its life. The drive is likely to be towards establishment of cohesion between members, to avoid competition and to placate the conductor.*

As with previous examples, these interventions all draw the group's attention to its interaction pattern, but vary in the extent to which they guide the group to consider a particular hypothesis in regard to this pattern. Some simply invite the group to explore their own interpretations of, or feelings concerning, the pattern; some introduce the notion that the pattern may serve the function of avoiding a problem for the group; and others indicate more directly what it is that may be being avoided. In regard to the latter, the therapists differ somewhat in their primary concerns. The most common focus is on the avoidance of feelings of greed and envy, but other concerns are the avoidance of loss of identity and of anger towards the therapist.

Other therapists are less concerned with interpreting the pattern than with indicating directly to the group that the pattern is less than optimally therapeutic; or with eliciting group members' dissatisfaction with it, even if this involves disclosing their own. Their interventions would have been as follows:

(M) If X continues pattern described say 'The cost of controlling spontaneity in this way is that real interaction doesn't develop and everyone is left wanting though secure. I would be surprised if this arrangement suits all members of the group.' (22)

Therapist notes – *1. New group, therefore fairly didactic intervention, pointing out conflict and compromise. 2. Last sentence intended as support for any prepared to speak their mind.*

(M) 'It seems to be safer to stay with your personal dramas than relate to each other. It's rather boring.' (23)

Therapist notes – *Appears to be a defensive stage fearing personal interaction. I would be profoundly bored after six sessions of this! (Counter transference or response). Expect my comment to produce some valid response, hopefully breaking the pattern. Responses of shock, fear, anger, something alive, here and now.*

(M) (I would have intervened a lot earlier than this.) (interrupt) (to X) 'Can you hold it for a minute?' (to group) 'This way we get to hear a lot about each person in turn and doubtless give good advice. But we aren't using the group to explore how we react to each other and feel about each other, which is in the long run going to be more useful.' (24)

Therapist notes – *Intervene to help establish different group culture.*

Despite the diversity of their interventions, there is also considerable commonality in our group analysts' reactions to the situation concerned. Virtually without exception, they imply in their notes, if not in the interventions themselves, that the turn-taking pattern is undesirable, and when they choose to intervene their interventions are, at least in part, directed towards the establishment of a more therapeutic pattern. In most cases, these interventions are focused upon the group as a whole rather than individual members, although in several instances concern that X should not feel rejected leads the therapist to make some reference to him. A final concern of many of the therapists is that, in a group which is at such an early stage of its development, interventions should be framed carefully if they are not to be unduly threatening to the group.

Chapter 5

A potential drop-out

David Kennard

SITUATION 3

The group is two months old. In the first few weeks two members dropped out without any discussion about leaving. Another member, John, has now missed two sessions without sending a message. In these two sessions members expressed some concern abut John's seeming to be depressed and socially isolated. At the next session John arrives a few minutes late. One member greets him cheerfully, 'Hello John, nice to see you.' Following this the other members proceed to talk about negative attitudes of work colleagues towards psychotherapy and to discuss in a rather intellectual way why people get depressed. Nothing is said to John, who remains silent.

THE THERAPIST'S TASK AND PROBLEMS

It is likely that most therapists would feel that their most important task in this session was to try to re-secure John as a member of the group. If he leaves it will be a double loss: John will lose out, and the group will suffer its third drop-out. Another aim, one which can be pursued at the same time, would probably be to help the group, which is still in its early stages, develop a therapeutic culture. By this it is meant that the members of a group develop attitudes, expectations, understandings, skills, etc. that work to promote the therapeutic value of the group for each of them, with the therapist facilitating or 'orchestrating' this process where necessary – hence the use of the term 'conductor'. The interaction – or lack of it – between John and the rest of the group is a natural focus for this aim. A third task for the therapist is to try to understand the processes occurring in the group at this point, and then judge to what extent it would be helpful to bring about awareness of these processes among its members – and how and when to do it.

Let us try to consider what processes may be going on here behind the visible interaction, in the 'invisible' group, as it were (see Agazarian and Peters, 1981, for more about this distinction). The short history of this group is clearly of some importance, for if John left the group he would be the third member to do so. The remaining members will of course be aware of this. What might they be feeling about it? Concern about John, but perhaps uncertainty over how to approach him, fearing that a direct question would upset him and make his departure even more likely. Concern also for the rest of the group: Will anyone else decide to leave? Will the group fall apart? Will the therapist decide to end the group? Perhaps too some annoyance at John for not contacting the group (through the conductor) to say he could not come. Might there also be around some wish that he *would* leave, that if he is not prepared to commit himself to coming each week – after all others in the group might also find it hard – it is better he should leave. This would leave more time for the ones who were left, and (in fantasy) the potential for a closer relationship with the therapist. Finally might there not also be some negative or mixed feelings towards the therapist about this situation: for not choosing members more carefully so as to avoid so many drop-outs, hoping or waiting for the conductor to tackle John over his absences and lateness.

Out of all this can be drawn certain issues or 'focal conflicts' (Whitaker, 1985) that the members may be experiencing, towards John, the group as a whole and the therapist. Towards John there appear to be two potential conflicts, one over what to do and the other over what to feel. The members want to find out how he is but do not want to risk upsetting him; and they may feel guilty over having driven him away in earlier sessions (by something someone said or failed to say) but annoyed with him over his apparent lack of commitment to the group. Towards the group, the members may feel that it is both a place of safety, a refuge from unsympathetic outsiders, but also a place that may potentially harm its members, e.g. by upsetting them. Towards the conductor the members may feel both positive expectations that he or she will 'know what to do', disappointment or anger in so far as he or she is seen as the person responsible for the problems besetting the group.

And what of John? Can we anticipate what he might be thinking or feeling? Apprehensive about the kind of reception he will get after two weeks' absence? (His lateness suggests he may be.) Holding on to the possibility that the group or the therapist can help him, but not sure how? Feeling guilt over not having been in contact? Feeling an outsider, not part of the group?

We can see, then, that underlying the apparently simple interaction described at the beginning of the chapter are a number of poignant issues. What are the therapist's options?

He or she can of course simply wait and see what develops in the group, and some of our respondents regard this as their first option. If the group continues like this till the end of the session, however, there is a chance that John may not return. If and when the therapist decides to intervene there are a number of choices. In the selection that follows the suggested interventions are grouped in a way that takes us through from those that aim to facilitate communication between John and the other members of the group, postponing exploration of the underlying meaning of the group's behaviour to a later occasion, to those that focus on prompting awareness of the underlying processes occurring in the group. As will be seen from the therapists' comments, the choice depends on the therapist's judgement of the members' capacity at this stage of the group to cope with an awareness of the presence of negative or mixed feelings: towards John, the therapist or the group itself.

While some respondents clearly favour concentrating on building a positive group atmosphere, others use this as an opportunity to teach the group something about the existence of unconscious links between unspoken preoccupations and overt topics of group conversation. Another choice concerns how confrontative to be – a wide range of approaches is evident, from warm encouragement and reassurance to 'laying it on the line'. Therapists have also varied in whether they address their remarks to John, the group as a whole or both. And perhaps the most important issue for many respondents has been judging the right balance between the therapist taking the lead in helping the group to overcome its difficulties, and enabling the members to discover their own capacity to deal with the situation. Group analysis as a method emphasises the importance of the group becoming the main agent of therapeutic change. Yet group analysts are sensitive to the needs of a group at a particular moment. In the interventions that follow we see experienced group analysts approaching this situation from many angles and making a wide range of decisions about these questions.

DIRECT APPROACH TO JOHN

(F) I would smile at John as he entered, possibly with a nod or gesture inviting him to sit down. At an appropriate stage I would address John: 'We had been wondering about your absence without any message. What happened?' I would restate reasons why regularity and punctuality are important (taking care not to sound like an ultimatum) AFTER he had given an answer and likely reactions from the group. (1)

Therapist notes – *At this early stage of the group a direct question to John seems preferable to asking the group's feelings about his absence/depression. Emphasise pleasure at his return rather than displeasure at his absence.*

This simple and direct intervention is well aimed. High on friendliness and warmth, low on threat, the therapist takes full responsibility for helping John to re-establish his presence in the group and uses this as an opportunity to do a spot of direct maintenance work on the group norms. The therapist deliberately decides not to address the underlying feelings or dynamics in the group, sensing that it is too early and that maintaining a positive, welcoming atmosphere is the most important thing right now. You feel that everything will be all right with this therapist. But will the group get the message that negative or difficult feelings are not to be brought into the open, and that members need not take any responsibility for the group?

ENCOURAGING THE MEMBERS THEMSELVES TO ASK JOHN ABOUT HIMSELF

(F) 'It seems difficult to speak to John about his absence and to tell him how you feel about him . . . after all you were worried about him . . .' (2)

Therapist notes – *I would wish to encourage free communication between the group members. In this case 'concern' for John would allow a positive beginning for further communication, it would encourage members to develop their feelings for one another, it would also point up their responsibility to one another over messages and so on.*

(F) 'It seems as if it is difficult for the group to tell John how concerned we were when he was away.' (3)

Therapist notes – *I would be wanting to confirm John's place in the group by letting him know that he was discussed when absent: not to be punitive about the absence: encourage the group to be potent and to engage John directly.*

(F) 'It seems hard to ask John why he has been away,' said with a smile at John in the hope that he will not feel this to be accusatory. (4)

Therapist notes – *Hoping to provoke discussion about fear that John might drop out, reassurance if his absence was for factual reasons, enable John to verbalise feelings about his difficulties in coming and to address the group's fears of having destroyed the members who dropped out.*

In slightly different ways these three therapists are trying to combine two things: bringing John into the group and helping the group to feel capable of taking responsibility for doing this. As with the first therapist there is still an emphasis on building a positive, non-punitive atmosphere, although the last therapist introduces the idea in her notes as to what part of the difficulty in talking to John may be: that the other members in some way feel that it is their fault that the two previous members dropped out of the group

CHALLENGING THE GROUP'S AVOIDANCE OF TALKING TO JOHN

Still focusing on opening up direct communication between John and the other group members, some of our respondents opted for a more challenging approach to the group by drawing attention to the relevance of the subject they are discussing to one of its own members.

(F) 'We are talking about the response of others – what about our own responses and concerns for each other here in the group?' (5)

(M) 'It seems we are more interested in external attitudes than our relations in the group. John has had the courage to return and is being ignored.' (6)

These interventions make their point clearly and directly but are likely to leave the group feeling reprimanded, something our other respondents were keen to avoid. Of course a lot depends on the tone of voice of the therapist. Take the following pithy intervention:

(M) 'We seem to having nothing to say to John on his return.' (7)

One could imagine this being said in a tart, disapproving voice, like a sharp rap over the knuckles (echoes of teacher looking for culprit: 'Nothing to say?'), or a warm, hopeful voice, inviting a response. The difference for the group would be enormous.

Therapist notes – *the intervention is an attempt to free the group to face feelings about John's absence, the departure of the two who dropped out, and each member's doubt about attending. John too may be enabled to speak.*

WONDERING ALOUD ABOUT THE GROUP'S BEHAVIOUR

In the following two interventions the therapist uses the approach of wondering aloud about the behaviour of the group. This implies that there is something to wonder about while leaving it up to the group members whether and how to respond.

(F) 'I wonder why no-one in the group is enquiring about John's absence. It seems to me that while he was away group members expressed some concern about him and yet now he is back no-one takes this up with him and I wonder what this means for the group.' (8)

Therapist notes –
1. *Don't do the work and make the enquiries, let the group do it.*
2. *Bring back into the group the missing bits and pieces, get all the unspoken thoughts under the psychotherapeutic umbrella.*
3. *Avoid more laborious interpretations re drop-outs, ambivalence about the group, etc. Hope it will come from the group – if not be ready to bring it in.*

(M) 'This has become a group where members' absence is a sensitive topic. You [the group] don't say anything about John missing two sessions and though others are pleased to see you [John] they haven't asked about your absence either.' (9)

Therapist notes – *I may be tempted to explore John's feelings and also the unfinished business concerning drop-outs.*

In using the 'wondering aloud' or 'just noticing things' technique the therapists are hoping to do two things: promote interaction between John and the other members and also to get the group thinking about what is happening in the group. Both interventions are made by therapists conscious of a connection between the overt topic of conversation and an underlying concern with John or with the matter of absences and drop-outs generally, but they do not refer to this directly – they simply indicate that they think there is a question to be addressed. This approach relies on the members' interest to carry it forward.

INTRODUCING THE NOTION OF PARALLEL COMMUNICATION IN A NON-SPECIFIC WAY

An alternative and quite deft approach to directing the members' attention towards what is happening within the group is to suggest to the group that, in effect, this is what they have been talking about anyway. It introduces the idea of parallel communication, described by Malan (1979), which is applicable to all forms of psychotherapy. This proposes that there is an underlying parallel between the issue or concern being openly talked about and another issue which the speaker (or in our case the group) is concerned about but is keeping out of awareness, presumably because of its troubling nature. Indeed the whole rationale of interpretation is based on the hypothesis of parallel meaning: it is one of the most fascinating aspects of psycho-analytically based work and also the one which most irritates (or threatens) its critics. Here are some interventions which suggest in the simplest manner (we will come to more elaborate interpretations further on) that parallel communication has been occurring. Here there is deliberately no attempt to say what the content of that communication might be, and in the terminology we have developed for our research these would be good examples of 'guided facilitation' in which the therapist opens a door into the parallel meaning but leaves it for the group to walk through.

(M) 'I wonder if we have been talking about our concern for John.' (10)

(M) 'Sounds as if the group are trying to express some concern about what's really been going on for John since he was last at the group. . .?' (11)

(M) 'I think members are speaking about John but not bringing him into it. Does anyone understand why?' (12)

(F) 'Could the general issues we are discussing be relevant to us in this room?'(13)

Such interventions, unlike the previous ones, are not invitations or suggestions that the group should do something (e.g. talk to John) but are, if you like, invitations to reflect on the group process. What is likely to be the effect on the group? Probably a rise in anxiety for those members who had been suppressing any thought for John and his predicament, but a sense of relief for any members who had been thinking about John but not saying anything. Making the link between the two parts of the parallel communication is always a delicate business as it implies that the group – or individual – did not actually know the full relevance of what was being said, a message which is often met with an initial response of disbelief or indignation, as a result of the interpretation being experienced as a narcissistically wounding attack rather than a helpful observation. One way to reduce the impact of this aspect of interpretative linking is to approach it rather like a teacher explaining how a piece of apparatus works. Note the way the third intervention, using the simple addition of a question, helps to reduce the interpretative sting by conveying the relative safety of a 'tutorial' atmosphere, while the fourth avoids specifically referring to John and has the following comment:

> Therapist notes – *I'd be demonstrating how a group can approach material – 'teaching-while-interpreting'. I'd be trying to look after John as an individual and the group as a whole by saying this.'*

EXPLICIT REFERENCE TO THE PARALLEL WITH MEMBERS' OWN NEGATIVE OR MIXED FEELINGS TOWARDS THE GROUP

In the following interventions the therapist goes one step further by suggesting that the negative attitudes towards psychotherapy which the group is talking about are indeed relevant to the concerns of the members themselves. They may hold such attitudes themselves and consequently feel quite ambivalent about the group. In this context John's absences and lateness, and the earlier drop-outs, raise a different issue for the group: not just the matter of expressing the group's concern directly to John, but that the extent to which there is ambivalence over whether to come to the group expresses something that other members are experiencing, i.e. their own uncertainty and mixed feelings about the group. In our examples so far the therapists, while aware of this issue, have opted to emphasise and build on positive feelings within the group, believing the group not yet ready to tackle underlying anxieties.

In the following interventions we see therapists seeking to balance the supportive and the exploratory, anxiety-raising aspects in the group. Getting this balance right is one of the most fundamental skills for any therapist, and it is interesting to see as we progress through our interventions how group analysts differ in the balance they select. Here two therapists raise this possibility in a fairly gentle way:

> (M) 'I wonder how everybody is feeling about the usefulness to them of being in this group.' (14)

> (F) 'It isn't easy at this early stage of the group to share one's doubts as to whether it is all worthwhile.' (15)

In the interventions that follow the therapists are more explicit.

(F) 'I'm beginning to wonder if people *in* the group share some of those negative attitudes to psychotherapy that we've been talking about. I've noticed that often when we talk about something outside the group it can be tied up with what people are feeling in the group – right now.' (16)

Therapist notes – *I think the group members may be holding back their own negative feelings about the group and possibly the conductor – also being afraid to express their own depression. As it is relatively early in the group's development I'd include a kind of teaching statement.*

(F) 'I think you may be talking about your own uncertain feelings about the group as well as your colleagues. Most people feel anxious early on in the group and it would be good to talk about it.' (17)

Therapist notes – *I think there is a fear that the group will collapse and that talking about this might make it happen, but because it is not talked about members feel isolated, each thinking the fear is a personal one. I would hope that John's absence and return would be taken up naturally within the ensuing discussion. If not I would find some way of doing this in the belief that he may be expressing the group's feelings.*

(M) 'Well I've been sitting here for the last couple of sessions trying to work out what's been going on behind the scenes in this group – and I feel it's got something to do with the very real doubts people often get after a couple of months in groups like this – you know – is this really going to work? I've done the wrong thing in coming here, etc.' (18)

Therapist notes – *I'd try to get the issue into the open and owned individually as a first step, then explore if possible how the group was dealing with this issue.*

(F) 'I wonder if by relating your work colleagues' opinions you actually express your own doubts about psychotherapy. You may wonder why two members left. Is John perhaps going to leave too? Do people leave because they get depressed in the group?' (19)

Therapist notes – *It seems to me that there are negative thoughts and feelings present which need to be expressed. The group is uncertain if this will be accepted. They may be afraid that addressing John directly asking him why he had missed two sessions and speaking their concern about his appearing depressed will upset him. They probably wonder if they said something to cause the other two to leave. Apparently the leaving has not been discussed before. This may be due to the conductor's own anxiety about discussing negative matters.*

(F) 'I think there is a lot of anxiety in the group about whether this therapy is going to work or not. Perhaps John expresses it by missing some sessions but I think he may not be the only person with mixed feelings.' (20)

Therapist notes – *In early group sessions I expect a universal anxiety (in the conductor too) about the group 'working' in every sense; about fear of group disintegration and fear of commitment. I prefer if possible to treat it as a group anxiety and also, if possible, I appeal to the 'adult' group – referring to our earlier agreed commitment to see things through.*

In these interventions the therapists go into and draw out a number of unexpressed thoughts and feelings that may be present amongst the members of the group: will it work? have I made the right choice? will it make us more depressed? have we said or done something to make people leave? In the way the interventions are made other points are also put across: the idea that behaviour such as missing a session can express an attitude; the reassurance that doubts about therapy are normal at this stage of a group and all right to talk about; the opportunity to make a general point about parallel communication.

In their notes the therapists also indicated some issues that they have not referred to in their interventions – e.g. members' fear that the group may collapse and doubts or negative feelings towards the therapist. Perhaps they judged that raising such matters directly would be too anxiety-provoking at this stage in the group. In terms of the development of the group norms, however, an implicit issue in many of the interventions has been who should take responsibility for dealing with the group's present predicament: the conductor or the group members? The following intervention puts this point clearly before the group.

(F) 'Last week there was a lot of concern about John, wondering what was keeping him away – yet today no one seems able to say anything to him. I think perhaps everyone feels a bit helpless and really expects me to deal with it and make the group feel a bit more comfortable.' (21)

Therapist notes – *There are two problems: John's absence and negative feelings towards the conductor. I think John needs to be helped to stay (hence letting him know he was missed last week) and the group needs to discover it can do this by talking to him, especially if two members have recently left.*

Far from increasing anxiety, this intervention appears sufficiently supportive and empathic to enable the group to recognise its dependency on the therapist in a way that will enable the members to start doing things for themselves. In contrast the following intervention makes similar points but in an entirely different tone:

(M) 'I am very concerned about what's going on. There seems to be an atmosphere of helplessness, as though psychotherapy is a waste of time and nothing is worth exploring. I think we should be concerned about the fact that John missed the last two sessions and was late today. Would you like to look at this John?' (22)

The opening statement that the therapist himself is 'very concerned' is indeed likely to raise the group members' anxiety considerably. The therapist conveys a certain franticness, for example both commenting on the atmosphere of the helplessness and then taking the lead in confronting John – thereby reinforcing the group's passivity. There is little sense of warmth or empathy, and the triple reference to helplessness, waste of time and nothing worth exploring feels just too demoralising. It feels as though the therapist himself believes the group is in trouble and that he has to go in firing on all cylinders to save it. There is quite a lot to be learned from a comparison of the above two interventions in terms of their similar intent and different delivery.

There remains one further area of 'hidden' feeling or communication within the group not yet commented on: that the group may be ambivalent not only towards group therapy and the therapist but also towards John. After all, does being depressed allow a member to disregard the expectation that members will contact the conductor if they are unable to attend? The other members have managed to struggle in in the face of whatever negative feelings they have about coming; if John isn't that committed better he leaves. Such thoughts are quite possible, but to voice them would seem hostile and uncaring in the circumstances: so, better just to ignore John for the moment. Two therapists grasped this particular nettle:

(F) 'The group got in touch with some of John's unhappiness last week but it seems no one knows quite what to do to help him now that he's here. Perhaps there are some mixed feelings about wanting to help him.' (23)

Therapist notes – *The phenomenon of drop-outs is clearly a group problem, i.e. no amount of support or encouragement from the conductor will prevent someone from dropping out if the group is pushing against or letting someone go. When groups do not respond with concern or anxiety to members dropping out, I assume that part of them wants the 'weaklings' out, the fantasy being that they will survive alone to be with the conductor.*

This is an interesting point, but it seems doubtful whether any of the members would be willing to acknowledge such mixed feelings so early in the group's life: that kind of interaction usually needs the group to feel safely solid and secure in its membership and leadership and both of these are 'in the air' at present. However a denial of the conductor's suggestion could serve to reunite John with the group, although at the expense of the conductor being cast in the role of spoiler. The conductor would then be acting as the repository of the group's negative feelings, which is a role the therapist must sometimes take. If the members did take up the point it would be important for the therapist to ensure that John got the message that this was a general issue for the group, and that sufficient personal support was expressed.

The following intervention must earn the award for the highest risk:

(M) 'It's a bit like the prodigal son isn't it? While John was away everyone was worried about him. Now when he comes back no-one knows whether they want to kill the fatted calf or kill John.' (24)

Therapist notes – *I'm offering a metaphor which allows more possibilities and levels of meaning than a straightforward interpretation. It's also a bit more dramatic, interesting and amusing (to me at least) and doesn't imply criticism of anyone. The group becomes a specific instance of a more or less universal human dimension.*

The reference to the prodigal son is apt but it assumes a knowledge of the relevant parable and a capacity to work with metaphor – the reference to wanting to kill John would be disturbing for a literal-minded group. While such an intervention could be stimulating for a special kind of group (say one composed of priests), it would be likely to throw most groups into some confusion as to what the therapist is getting at, and runs the risk of making the members feel that something clever is being said at their expense.

TECHNICAL CONSIDERATIONS: NON-VERBAL COMMUNICATION AND DELAYED INTERVENTIONS

Two aspects of the interventions have been left till last. Both concern matters of technique, timing and tactics. The first is the use of non verbal communication from the conductor to the group. Some of our therapists sought to facilitate communication between John and the rest of the group in this way, allowing the group's conversation to unfold without interruption. In one case this was the sole intervention:

(M) I would watch John closely, making it plain to anyone watching that I was doing so. (25)

Therapist notes – *I would hope that my close observation of John would lead someone in the group to bring him into the interaction, linking the conversation to him. I would prefer not to make my own input at this stage, hopefully the group would make the connection. If the situation persisted an intervention would be appropriate.*

For other therapists a non-verbal communication was the first of a two- or three-part intervention.

(M) I should be endeavouring to make eye contact with John to signal enquiry and invitation. If that failed. . . (26)

(F) I would make occasional eye to eye contact with John, in an encouraging way, hoping to stimulate him to speak. I would allow the group to continue for a while in the hope that someone might turn to John. (27)

Those therapists whose initial intervention was in the form of a non-verbal communication, to John or the group, tended to have a rather clear plan in mind, moving from such minimal interventions to more direct approaches if the group did not make the connections for itself. This introduces the second and important technical point, that of delaying an intervention until it either becomes unnecessary – because the group has made the connection – or necessary because the group seems unlikely to make the connection at this stage without any help. These 'paced' interventions have been quoted in part and are now given in full for the insight they give into some of the tactical aspects of group analysis.

(M) I should be endeavouring to make eye contact with John to signal enquiry and invitation. If that failed I might say: 'It seems easier to talk about depression than to admit that some of us may be depressed. We seem to be ignoring the meaning of John's absence these last two weeks.' (26)

Therapist notes – *I see John (and the two who have left) expressing the group ambivalence to therapeutic work and their difficulty opening up their disappointment, anger and fear. I want them, and John too, to see how his absence speaks for them all.*

(F) I would make occasional eye to eye contact with John, in an encouraging way, hoping to stimulate him to speak. I would allow the group to continue for a while in the hope that someone might turn to John. I would not wait longer than 20 minutes to half an hour (*maximum*) and would then say if the group had not developed along these lines – 'Our concern about whether other people think therapy helpful or not must have some connection with your feelings about X and Y's leaving, and John's absence for two weeks, and also your own doubts about group psychotherapy.' The group without doubt will then pick up at least one of these points and I would help them to explore their feelings. If necessary I would be prepared to focus again on any of these three points not discussed, but would not interrupt valuable work – I would 'hold it' for later. I would hope John would speak with or without help from the group, if not I would turn to him and say, 'the group expressed their concern when you were away about how depressed you had looked.' (27)

Therapist notes – *Obviously it is better if the group can do it for themselves. If not, my prime responsibility as a conductor is to focus on the most important areas (but not to make lengthy interpretations at this point). There is a need for John to speak if he is to be held in the group, and this is facilitated usually if he knows his depressed state has been perceived and that the group cares. In both these interventions I would hope the approach and phrasing could serve as a model for group members to follow on future occasions (well sometimes!).*

Foulkes (1964, pp. 62–3) has observed that it is the job of the conductor to lead at the start, but to allow the group to take him or her off a pedestal when it no longer needs him or her there. So the therapist moves from being the leader of the group to the leader in the group. Throughout this chapter we have seen therapists approaching this central issue from several directions, and with varying judgements about where the balance should be struck between allowing the group to discover its own capacity to take responsibility and the responsibility of the therapist for the group's welfare and in particular the welfare of a vulnerable member. This has been a particularly rich set of interventions to one situation, ranging widely from supportive holding to challenging interpretations. Few if any of these interventions would have been unproductive. Perhaps what stands out most is that there are not many aspects of a group's experience that cannot be opened up within the group if the way of doing this is relaxed, empathic and encouraging.

Chapter 6

A member seeks approval for concurrent individual therapy

David A. Winter

SITUATION 4

This group has been meeting for a year. An attractive young woman (one of five siblings) has, after a difficult start in which she tended to be a monopoliser, apparently settled in and become a rather more integrated group member. You are nevertheless aware that she has intense and unresolved problems of rivalry with her mother in relation to her father. Today she announces, with coy hesitation, that she is sure the group is going to be very angry with her because she has, unbeknown either to them or to her female group therapist, been seeing a male psychotherapist on an individual basis for the past six months. The group respond warmly and supportively to her disclosure, commend her for her courage in making it, and encourage her to continue to make use of both therapeutic modalities. She turns to you and asks prettily if you mind.

THE THERAPIST'S TASK AND PROBLEMS

To begin by considering this young woman's question, would her therapist be likely to mind that she has been secretly undergoing individual psychotherapy? Certainly, the arrangement of concurrent group and individual psychotherapy is not unknown, and Foulkes was not altogether averse to offering individual sessions to group members, although generally not without consideration of such aspects of requests for individual sessions as the oedipal conflicts which they might reflect (Foulkes and Anthony, 1957). Amongst the reasons for offering individual therapy to a group member may be to support him or her through a life crisis or to facilitate his or her effective participation in the group. However, as Yalom (1985) notes, drawbacks of such arrangements are that the client may avoid the expression of affect in the group by reserving it for the individual sessions; and that the group and individual therapist, if these are not the same person, may work at cross purposes. In his view, in order for individual and group psychotherapy to complement each other, the two therapists must be in frequent communication, and the individual therapy should be focused on the client's experience of the group.

The therapist in the example, even if not being entirely opposed to the notion of concurrent individual and group psychotherapy, is therefore at the very least likely to be concerned about the way in which the individual therapy has been arranged and the six months of secrecy about it, and she may possibly wish to communicate with the individual therapist. If she is not in agreement with concurrent therapies, she might conceivably wish to present the client with the ultimatum of pursuing either one or the other therapeutic modality. In either instance, the therapist will have to face the issues of whether to convey her displeasure to the client, and how to put into effect any arrangements which may ensure the complementarity of the two approaches or the discontinuation of one of them. Her approach to these matters may be influenced by a wish to convey some approval of the client's decision to disclose her secret to the group. In deciding whether it is appropriate to express any displeasure which she feels, she may also take into consideration the extent to which this may reflect any of her insecurities as a therapist and consequent feeling that the client has rejected her therapeutic efforts in favour of the male therapist.

Quite apart from such issues relating to the manifest content of the client's question, the therapist is also likely to wish to explore various areas concerning the meaning of this question and of the client's disclosure. Why, for example, did she initially seek out individual psychotherapy? How did her decision to do so relate to her 'intense and unresolved problems of rivalry with her mother in relation to her father'? Is it significant in this regard that her group therapist is female and that she has found a male individual therapist? Is it significant that she had initially tended to monopolise the group? How does she expect the therapist to react to her disclosure? How does she expect the group to react? How does she wish them to react?

A final issue on which the therapist might choose to focus is the apparently supportive way in which the group has, in fact, reacted to the revelation. Is what they are supporting the challenge which she has made to the therapist's authority and her implied message that the help provided by the group is insufficient to meet members' needs? Are they simply relieved that she has an alternative therapeutic resource in that this might make her less likely to monopolise the group once again? Will they begin to consider whether individual psychotherapy might also be of benefit to them? And, if so, does the therapist need to intervene in such a way as to stem any tide of potential defections to individual therapy? As well as the positive feelings which they have expressed towards the client, might they also harbour as yet unrevealed resentments concerning her disclosure? Could it be that they are not fully aware of some of these feelings?

Given these many facets of the problem which the client has posed, which particular issue should be the therapist's primary concern? Should her intervention be primarily directed towards the maintenance of optimal therapeutic conditions for the client concerned and for the group as a whole? Or should the latent content of the client's actions, and of the group's reaction to these, be her initial focus of exploration? Are these two possible foci of an intervention necessarily mutually exclusive? Let us see how some of our sample of group analysts would have responded if faced with this situation.

SELECTED INTERVENTIONS

(M) 'Yes.' (1)

Therapist notes – *It would need later to be unravelled. Suspect the group would be angry with me.*

Very rarely does a group analyst make such a direct and bald statement of how he or she feels about an issue. It is important to note that this therapist qualifies his response with the statement that he would only make it if he felt that the client was 'cohered'.

This was not the only therapist who would be prompted by this situation to reveal how he feels about the client's disclosure. However, the other therapists who indicate that they would tell the client that they do mind would also convey the reasons for their displeasure. Their responses were as follows:

(F) 'Yes I do mind because you left it so long before telling us. I am wondering what my irritation is about otherwise. I am aware that I am a woman and your other therapist is a man. You must have realised that interactions with other members could assist your analysis inside the group yet you chose a male therapist rather than a man in the group. Therapists are special people for you. I sense that you challenge me with this information and that you are supported by your siblings in the group.' I could make reference to her past triangular relationships or leave her to do so according to what is already apparent to the group. (2)

(M) 'Yes I do mind. Not because you are trying to get your father's attention as well as your mother's, that is only natural, but because you are creating the same split here as happened at home in doing it this way. You even expect us to be angry.' (3)

Therapist notes – *Be honest and interpret. If needed also interpret group denial.*

These therapists are not only telling the client that they mind what she has done, but also drawing attention to parallels, in the second case by means of an interpretation and in the first somewhat less directly, between her actions and her family situation. As well as focusing on the client's disclosure, the first therapist makes reference to the group's reaction to it, while the second indicates that he might also do so.

Other therapists, while being aware that they would be angry with the client, are concerned at what might be the effects of any direct expression of this anger in response to the client's question.

They responded thus:

(M) I would of course be angry and feel threatened. If I retained enough presence of mind, I would say, not to her but to the group, 'I can understand anyone needing to feel special in the group but there is a problem if it is achieved at the expense of commitment to the group.' (4)

Therapist notes – *I would be tempted to deliver some crushing personal interpretation to the young woman. It would be safer and more appropriate to put it into a group context and to help members to confront her and themselves with their feelings.*

(M) (1) I'd have to sit on my real anger quite hard, initially, as it would be counter-productive to express it directly!
(2) I'd wait hopefully for the group to make this interpretation. When they failed to, I'd make some very simple but direct intervention on the lines of 'I wonder if the mother-group isn't feeding you enough', and be prepared to elaborate on what I meant by this, if the client or group feign incomprehension. (5)

Therapist notes – *Wow, where have I gone wrong? Why aren't the group dealing with it? I don't use a lot of straightforward 'analytic' interpretations in this culture, but in a case like this an extended bit of interpretation will be required.*

It may be that it is the extent of these two therapists' anger with the client which causes them to be concerned about its possible effects. It is of interest that, in their initial reactions to the client's question, they both take a course directed towards helping the group to take the responsibility of confronting her with their less positive feelings, and their interpretations, concerning her actions.

Other therapists would react to the client's question by revealing not their feelings regarding the client's individual therapy but their feelings regarding her decision to disclose this. Their responses would be as follows:

(M) 'I'm pleased that you've told me about this. I wonder what stopped you mentioning it before and why it became possible today.' (6)

Therapist notes – *The patient has challenged the therapist and is expecting to be criticised/told off. It is important not to fall into this trap, but to explore it with her. I would also be thinking about how to deal with other members' enthusiastic reaction, which seems very much a denial of their envy.*

(F) 'It is good to think you can now share this with us.' (7)

Therapist notes – *To enable her to feel she is accepted by all and can go on to explore her unresolved problems.*

For some therapists, their response to the client's question, at least initially, would not be to reveal whether they mind but to adopt the trusty therapeutic ploy of facilitating further exploration of the client's feelings, and in particular her expectations and wishes concerning the therapist's reactions to her disclosure, by reflecting her question back to her. For example:

(M) 'What do you think?'
If no reply from her, or response from the group members I might say: 'I'm glad you told us, but as it took six months I wonder if you were afraid I'd mind, as though I was your mother objecting to you having the relationship you wanted with your father.' (8)

or

(F) A direct, I hope warm, questioning long look – pause – 'Do you want me to mind?' (9)

Therapist notes – *I'd rather she explored her fantasies about my response than give it immediately. (I might later.) On the whole I prefer to 'use' the transference rather than 'interpret' it. If she won't, I think the group would or could lead onto the way they encourage her to act out their own wishes.*

(M) Raised eyebrows would indicate surprise and a hint of disapproval.
'You thought we would be angry?'
and later:
'It is going to be very important that your other therapist and I keep close contact with each other. May I telephone him from time to time?' (10)

Therapist notes – *The expectation of anger gives access to her difficulty sharing. The triangle of the two therapists with herself offers a continuing forum for replay of her early difficulty with her mother – a strong 'bond' between the 'parents' in the new drama will be helpful.*

The last two examples illustrate that the non-verbal components of a therapist's intervention may be as important as the words that are used. In the second of these, it is also noteworthy that the delayed part of the intervention serves two functions. The therapist here is paving the way for practical arrangements which may ensure that the concurrent therapies proceed in complementary fashion, and is doing so in a way which is intended to provide a 'corrective emotional experience' in which relationships within the triangle of the two therapists and her are more satisfactory than they were in her earlier triangle with her parents. It is clear, however, that in some cases the group therapist's discussions with the individual therapist are likely to be less than amicable. Consider, for example, the notes made by one of the therapists concerning her intervention:

Therapist notes – *I feel very angry with the individual therapist, assuming he was party to the arrangement of dual therapy. In any case I would be seeking to gain permission to speak to him and if it was denied by the patient would make it clear that I thought the situation was detrimental to her and the group.*

Some therapists would indicate to the client that they are not going to answer her question because there are other, more pressing, questions which need to be considered. For example:

(F) 'The question is not whether I mind. The question is what does it mean to you to have two therapies, one you share with the group and another that remained secret, kept away from us. Are you getting more or less than the rest of the group?' (11)

Therapist notes – *My aim is to make her and the group explore the negative sources and the negative effects of her apparent advantage, namely her acting out her envy, rivalry, destructiveness in relationships, betrayal of the group and its conductor, and finally the group's complete denial of their resentment with her.*

(M) 'You appear rather seductive. It's not a question of what I mind. It is a question of what you and the group are involved in.' (12)

Therapist notes – *Responding to the existential drama; the girl representing the oedipal dynamic in the group involving me, conductor (father) and the group collusion. I would also ask question why the oedipal group was not angry with the girl. It seems a covert dynamic has been operating for six months and I had either missed it, been ineffectual, or both. Would hope for an interesting group.*

(F) 'It isn't a question of whether I mind or not. It is a question of whether you have jeopardised your therapy with us here firstly by your decision to begin a separate therapy and then to withhold this important decision from us for six months.' (13)

Therapist notes – *I would certainly feel hurt and angry and would have to concentrate on containing those feelings. However, with such a serious boundary issue, I am sure I would be quite active in trying to sort something out. I am not sure that I would be prepared to continue seeing a patient under these circumstances. Much would depend on the patient's capacity to understand the underlying meaning of her actions and my ability to form a constructive link with her other therapist. My experience of patients who are working with two 'competing' therapists indicates that it's not always in the interests of patients to proceed. Somehow my comments to this patient would have to indicate the seriousness of her acting out in order to fully elicit her co-operation in repairing the situation.*

For another therapist, it is clear that the situation can only be repaired by the client opting for either one therapy or the other. He does not hesitate to say so, although couching his remarks in a supportive, non-condemnatory manner:

(M) 'It is understandable that you have taken out the 'insurance' of two therapies, but you'd get more out of concentrating on one and choose before the session and come to it ready to discuss your choice.' I might try to connect with earlier oedipal feelings if appropriate. (14)

Therapist notes – *Transference diluted and participation split or warped by two depth (i.e. transferential) psychotherapies. It's important to do the above in a tolerant enabling manner – not rejected or slighted way.*

Other therapists seem more prepared to accept that the concurrent therapy arrangement may not be inappropriate for this particular client. For example:

(F) 'My first thought is that you have been having an easier time in the group recently and I wonder if your individual therapy has been helping you here too. I must admit I am a bit startled that you have been in individual therapy for six months and haven't told us before. Have you perhaps been worried that we might resent it?' (15)

Therapist notes – *My immediate emotional response could be irritation but there is of course no reason why she should not have both individual therapy and group therapy – the first task is to understand the need to keep them separate and not to get caught on the projective identification of a rivalrous mother and replay the past.*

Some therapists appear largely to ignore the client's question and instead attend either to the facilitation of exploration of the issues which the client's disclosure has raised or to interpretations of the client's actions. First, a very open facilitatory remark designed to elicit further reactions from the group:

(F) 'I think we should talk about it in the group.' (16)

Therapist notes – *A direct response will elicit any anger there is in the group which I can then interpret. It puts the therapy clearly on the agenda and gives me time to think and collect more information.*

Next, two facilitatory interventions which are guiding the client in a particular direction, namely the exploration of parallels between her present situation and her past experiences:

(F) 'I have a feeling that there is something which may seem familiar in your situation, and that you seem to be expecting that I might mind, or be angry with you.' (17)

Therapist notes – *I would be 'feeling my way' at this stage – a heavy transference interpretation would be tantamount to retaliation, i.e. that I 'minded'.*

Although this therapist is 'feeling her way', she also probably has a fairly clear idea of what the similarities might be between the client's present and past situations. However, she chooses not to express this idea directly as an interpretation, which she fears might have punitive connotations, but rather to nudge the client gently in the direction of exploring these similarities.

The next therapist also employs a facilitatory intervention, but this time one which, with the aid of a simile, guides the client rather more directly towards consideration of the parallels between her situation in the group and that in her family of origin:

(F) 'I think it feels to you that the group is like a cake and that there are never enough pieces to go round. Is this the way it has always been for you?' (18)

And finally, a more interpretative intervention which addresses not only how the client's behaviour relates to her childhood experiences but also what function it serves for the group:

(F) 'I think that you may be acting out a childhood wish-fantasy for the whole group about having a special relationship with one parent to the exclusion of everyone else. By setting up this situation you are repeating a childhood problem rather than resolving it.' (19)

Therapist notes – *Though there is a lot more to say, I trust the group to do the rest, to avoid a repetition of a young woman's struggle with me as her mother.*

This therapist chooses to interpret, while also acknowledging that there is more that she could have said. She, and many of the other therapists in the examples which we have presented, provide good illustrations of the fact that group analysts will often be aware of many more feelings and hypotheses concerning situations in their groups than they are prepared to reveal. As we have seen, a primary consideration of a number of the therapists, in deciding to what extent to convey their feelings and views regarding the client's individual psychotherapy, has been the concern not to react in a way which is likely to repeat the pattern of the client's past relationships with her parents.

Chapter 7

An invitation to a Christmas party

Jeff Roberts

SITUATION 5

It is the last session before the Christmas break in a group that has now been meeting for a year. The members have been unable, in spite of much hard work on your part, to accept their denial of anxiety over the impending separation – in fact they all appear extremely cheerful. On this occasion one member brings in unexpectedly a basket, full of home-made mince-pies, which smell delicious, and another member a bottle of wine and glasses for everyone, including the therapist.

THE THERAPIST'S TASK AND PROBLEMS

The members of this group can be said to have become involved in a manic flight and are intent upon establishing 'a manic feast'. They appear to be denying the significance of losing a contact with the group for the Christmas break and are setting out in a collusive way to prevent any meaningful discussion of the darker side of Christmas. The protagonists have arranged a piece of collective acting in,[1] and at the moment when an intervention is asked for it seems likely that all members of the group will join in.

If the conductor allows this apparently innocent celebration to proceed he or she will be effectively disabled from making remarks which might be seen as ungrateful or unpleasant in view of the celebratory atmosphere which the members are providing. The group is thus flouting the agreed rules of abstinence of the 'analytic context' and in fact, I believe, manifesting considerable aggression towards the conductor.

The task of the conductor is initially that of observing the group and becoming aware of the pattern of events. He or she will almost certainly have the rather unpleasant sensation that something quite powerful is happening, whose meaning is unclear but which implies that in some way he or she has lost control of the group. Out of this, if the conductor is familiar with the language of psychoanalysis, will come the idea that the group is acting out (or acting in). The group is denying any feelings of loss and substituting for these actions symbolic of joy and celebration. In being unable to resist the impulse to act on their feelings the members of the group are also breaking the rules of abstinence which are fundamental to the psychoanalytic process. Instead of striving to put feelings, fantasies and thoughts into words, which is the task of the group, a collective decision has been made to enact a celebration. The conductor has two pressing tasks. One is to reach a hypothesis about the meaning of this behaviour. The second is to come quickly to a decision as to how best to manage it. He or she has about as long as it takes to open a bottle to come up with an initial intervention.

One of the considerations of the conductor will be, on the one hand, how to manage the situation and, on the other, not deal out a gratuitous narcissistic wound to those who have so generously brought food and drink to the group. Is there an unnoticed reference to communion here? In which case the group is paradoxically confusing Christ's birthday with the celebration of his death and resurrection. Indeed it could be suggested that in its mode of celebrating a beginning it is unwittingly celebrating the ending which it so much wishes to avoid.[2] It is important that he or she attempts to re-establish an abstinent environment in which an analysis of acting out can occur. Through this it may be possible to get in touch with the current experience of loss in the group and thereby past experiences of loss. The mood might then become that of sadness and depression rather than gaiety and excitement.

The conductor would also do well to consider that there has been a significant loss of boundaries in the group, which he or she should not collude with if he or she is not to allow a precedent for similar acting in or acting out in the future.

SELECTED INTERVENTIONS

(F) 'I would probably wait to see how the group developed before saying anything – and then say I think the group want to avoid the difficult feelings to do with separation and the Xmas holiday by having a party instead.' (1)

or in a similar vein but more concisely:

(F) 'P and G are out to help us avoid the empty feelings of parting.' (2)

In both these cases the conductors have allowed the 'acting in' to continue. They have been tactful in relation to the donors and also made an intervention which draws attention to the probable underlying motivation. They have not addressed the aggressive or attacking quality of this kind of activity (indeed few of our conductors do this). They have both made a judgement about the kind of feelings engendered by parting. Indeed conductor 2 has been somewhat transparent in indicating that parting is for her accompanied by 'empty feelings'. Undoubtedly breaks are painful and difficult times but those who have enjoyed Christmas at home and have been involved in long school terms will know that some partings can also involve joyful feelings.

(M) 'If it was Easter coming up I'd think this was the "last supper", but as it's time for a virgin birth maybe it's a fertility rite we've got here.' (3)

Therapist notes – *There's no point going on doing what hasn't been working. It will only lead to them doing more of what they've been doing so it's up to me to come at it from a completely different angle. I've introduced the break and addressed the meal and anxiety about impending loss and the possibility of new life and maybe the loss of virginity: but not in a way that tells them which bit to respond to or gives them any indication how to respond but I hope it's a strange and evocative enough statement for it to be difficult for them to ignore it. It's also a statement I enjoy making so I get out of the trap of working hard and getting nowhere and becoming irritated and fed up. [He continues] I often bring up the theological significance of Christmas and Easter (only of course when the majority of the members of the group share this culture). It's something however that everyone knows at some level and is part of our shared unconscious process of reality construction; part of the foundation matrix.[3]*

This therapist has chosen to attack the acting out by intervening in a way which will puzzle the members, at the same time attempting to engage the group by addressing its unconscious through metaphor. If a well-chosen metaphor is used as an intervention at the right moment it can have profound therapeutic effects. The language of metaphor is more akin to the language of the unconscious than is everyday speech. Often, for instance, dreams speak in metaphorical language. Metaphors can encompass a situation in a more accurate and economical way than extended and elaborate description and explanation in 'digital' language. Murray Cox, who has written a book on metaphor in psychotherapy with Alice Thielgaard (Cox and Thielgaard, 1987), proposes that metaphors can promote deep changes without disturbing the surface. They can act rather like a depth charge.

(M) 'My face would signal surprise and a wry pleasure. I would eat and drink with them. I might say, at some point, "Parting party?", or perhaps refer to the communion of the last supper.' (4)

Therapist notes – *I regard 'acting in' as an acceptable form of communication, as deserving of attentive listening as the spoken word. I think it is possible to overstate the significance of breaks and to ignore the relief and opportunity a break can bring. Fun as well as gloom belongs in groups.*

This is enormously seductive. There is a positive element to the end of term, representing as it does the completion of a period of work and the beginning of a time of leisure. But breaks in therapy as in life can have destructive effects on relationships and on the therapeutic process. Breaks, particularly if not talked about, can lead to drop-outs, exacerbations of symptoms, suicidal behaviours and all kinds of acting out. The acting out may also be more likely in those groups in which acting in has been permitted and the darker side of the Christmas feelings not allowed expression in the group. Also if the conductor overtly or covertly permits or encourages this behaviour it will become embedded in the culture of the group and acting in and out will persist for the life of the group. Moreover it will not always be as containable and harmless as that seen in this vignette.

(F) 'You know that you come to this group for what we understand as 'therapy'. If we were meeting as friends the pies and wine would be delightful but we must understand why the group 'needs' this party and then perhaps after the group is over we may feel that it is OK to join together in food and drink.' (5)

Therapist notes – *I would wish to insist on seeking to understand the meaning of everything said and done in relation to the group. Here the anxiety over the impending break is being defended. I feel it can be clarified without causing pain to those wishing to party. It is, of course, an attack on my authority but this can be picked up after the break. I would not join in the party after the group.*

This intervention is an unequivocal attempt to maintain the boundaries of the group and to maintain a state of therapeutic abstinence within the communicational field of the group. The therapist has clearly stated boundaries and her determination to maintain them. It seems to me also to be a simple non-interpretative encouragement to the group to use its resources to explore the meaning behind its behaviour. Undoubtedly, however, those who wish to party will experience pain, although it would not be correct for the therapist to identify his or herself as the primary cause of this pain, which has in fact been imported concealed by the Christmas goodies.

There is an interesting additional issue arising from the therapist's decision not to join the party after the group. It poses the question as to where the party should now be held. Not allowing the party, if still desired, to happen in the final five minutes of the group (the therapist can decide whether to join in or not) may turn acting in into acting out, in which the stifled merriment is carried off perhaps to the home of one of the members.

(M) 'The funeral meats seem to have become the wedding treats.' (6)

Therapist notes – *Having been trained by the late Jim Home, I find myself very often commenting in a slightly oblique manner (not as a fad!) which I believe allows each individual to stop and try and find his/her meaning about the comment.*

I would regard the above scene as an avoidance of pain of separation and feel bound to communicate what seems difficult to express.

This conductor is determined that his group will work to find the meaning in their behaviour. I am uncertain about commenting on this. One must assume a group well trained in the conductor's approach which will use what he has offered and, in an authentic group-analytic way, be derailed from their intention to act in and return to analysis of the group by the group including the conductor. A lot depends, I think, on whether this intervention goes over their heads or hits them below the belt. In the latter case it is likely to be successful. My problem is I have never heard of 'wedding treats' and 'funeral meats'. If I were a group member would I just let this pass or would I put down the corkscrew and ask for clarification?

(F) 'I would sit tight and say/do nothing. Towards the end of the group, assuming mince-pies eaten and wine drunk, I might encourage the group to look at ending. OR I would direct the group to wait till the end – but I doubt this.' (7)

Therapist notes – *I don't think it's helpful to instruct people to give up their resistance – the group is too young, and I do not yet understand how the separation process is working.*

This therapist has chosen a minimal intervention. She has a point but is taking a risk since it is easier to open a door than to close it again. Allowing 'acting in' to occur sets a precedent and lets a group know for all time that their conductor has a permissive style.

Example: a long-standing group (at the Group-Analytic Practice) was taken over by a new conductor. It was the last group of the week and clearly the previous conductor had relaxed a little in this group, looking forward to some free time ahead. The group had cigarette smokers actively smoking in the group and routinely helped itself to coffee from the staff kitchen. Wine was drunk to celebrate the departing conductor's exit. Five years on, despite a complete turnover of personnel, including the second conductor, the group still routinely helps itself to coffee from the staff kitchen. No other group at the Practice does this!

(M) I would avoid eating or drinking, though I would comment on how good it looked and smelt. 'It's as though we are at your home – just dropped in – perhaps one of us is Father Christmas, Christmas is such a hospitable time. It's as if the group is already having a break and is throwing mud in the face of its own tradition and custom.' (8)

Therapist notes – *I would not wish to appear to accept the gifts thus favouring one or two members, whom I suspect are the group's most consistent deniers. I would want to focus on the family aspect of Christmas, or the remeeting of friends – in contrast to this group 'family' here. I would hope that the group would go further and associate about gifts, Father Christmas, Messiahs and feelings about the group, perhaps 'no room at this inn!'*

This therapist is very clear about what he desires his group to think about. He is here choosing not to accept the advice which Wilfred Bion (Bion, 1970) gave to psycho-analysts, namely 'to go into each session without memory or desire'. He has admirable hopes for his group's agenda and yet my personal tendency is to side with Bion, feeling that expectations and desires can lead to disappointment, promote unauthentic expression and stifle genuine creativity.

So far I have only considered this conductor's commentary on his intervention, which I think is not only a powerful intervention but also makes me feel rather uncomfortable. The conductor is clear over his boundary issues and initially (apparently) quite generous in his appreciation of the gifts. This intervention, however, has an enormous sting in its tail. It confronts the aggressiveness of the acting out head on. I am not able to come down clearly on the side of gentleness or confrontativeness as the best approach in this case. This particular intervention will be very painful for the group to receive. Will it give them food for thought and bring them up short? Will it give them yet another wound to lick and generate useless hostility towards the therapist? One powerful retaliation for a wound received in the final group of the term is not to return for the next.

(F) I would not reject the 'Christmas gift' outright, but would say 'Before drowning your sorrows in drink, there's a lot of work for us to do. Parties, especially at Christmas time, almost always entail pain, even if it is difficult to reach. The mince-pies smell delicious, but are not really the answer to emotional hunger, except as a brief palliative. Let's look at what's going on beneath the cheerful surface.' If silence followed I'd say 'It's difficult to let go the cheerfulness – sadness is painful.' (We'd probably still have the food after the session.) (9)

Therapist notes – *My comments would focus on loss – pain and sadness (not anger at first due to the denial); I find sadness easier to access than anger. I might later suggest that there was 'disappointment' that the group would not be meeting for some weeks, but we would be unlikely to reach anger for a while (and no doubt this will lead to strong repercussions after the break). 'Let's look at' is a very useful type of intervention and again emphasizes the group's responsibility for (and ultimately the greater value to them of) finding their own interpretation. I would not reject the culinary offering (as it had already been produced) for to do so could be experienced as rejection by the patients. However only after its significance had been analysed would I allow consumption (and then it should be at the end of the session). I would decline the alcohol and tell the group I had work to do still.*

This therapist has developed a clear hypothesis about what's going on and communicates this to the group with great clarity and at some length; she eschews pithy metaphorical communication and is very much focusing on the here and now. Moreover she demonstrates a degree of therapeutic tact and respect for the feelings of her group which some of our other therapists appear to find unnecessary and perhaps undesirable. Once again we have arrived at a dilemma concerning what degree of confrontativeness and respect, or lack of respect, for the feelings of one's patients is ultimately in their best interest. The following is another example of a male therapist being quite unkind in the way he undermines the party spirit.

(M) 'Ah! Cheerful to the last. . .thank you, yes I will have a mince-pie. . .

delicious!. . .something extra, something special today. . .but next week [with irony]. . .nothing!' I would carry on interpreting the denial and the mince-pies as acting out, but without attacking the action itself. (10)

Therapist notes – *I would not want to attack the acting out, which takes a constructive form, but to interpret it, and keep the group in touch with the denied negative aspect of the transference.*

This therapist is confident and clear in his decision to allow the acting out to continue and an intention to attack the denial. He does not believe that only by depriving the group, at least initially, of the gratification it is seeking will words become available to describe the feelings. It could be argued that this is not so and that words and actions are mutually exclusive alternatives. This would support those therapists who attempt to prevent the action and encourage the group to find their feelings and then to find some words with which to understand these feelings. However, it is not so very easy to prevent a piece of acting out from happening. It is possible to sympathise with the discomfort and even despair of the following therapist, knowing that one has had similar experiences.

(M) 'Well – I feel utterly shocked inside (with a sort of comfortable detachment from the counter-transference). We've been meeting as a serious group all year, and it's just disappeared, and been replaced with all this, I feel quite devastated.' (11)

Therapist notes – *(This happened to me, I didn't handle it well. Thanks for the second chance.) This group is unable to contain the separation anxiety, denying and projecting it into the therapist – shock, loss, impotence, devastation etc. I would hold this position, claiming to be too devastated to even join in the festivities and although physically present would be unable emotionally to come to the party.*

Pontius Pilate is alive and well and living in   . I think that in this piece of self-disclosure this therapist is honestly acknowledging the true dreadfulness of all the dilemmas the group has so cheerfully imposed on him. He experiences a powerful and complex projective process and, although wanting to do it better this time, seems to be setting up a situation in which he identifies with the projection. This seems to me unlikely to turn things round on the night and may leave the group members with some quite nasty guilt to take away with them.

(M) 'Well they smell delicious, I suppose this must be something like a wake. Perhaps though we should eat them after the group time is over.' (12)

Therapist notes – *I don't see anything wrong with the food and drink in themselves but they can be used to generate discussion of the underlying issues.*

This therapist, in contrast to the previous ones, takes it all very calmly and, although postponing the acting out, does it gently and has chosen to use a metaphorical approach to attempt to gain access to unconscious processes.

(F) Initially nothing – I'd wait and see how the session unfolded hoping that the group would begin, through acting out, to explore its own manic defences. If not I would draw a comparison between a relevant situation and this, e.g. a wake after a funeral or the Christmas rush and a desire to bring lots of goodies and presents as a cover for much of the distress and pain that people are aware of. (13)

Therapist notes – If the group has reached the last session so resistant to exploring their anxiety, I don't think that coming down on them like a ton of bricks with the obvious interpretation that they're denying the anxiety and turning it into a party would be 'heard'. However I think acting out often does lead to insight through a recognition of how difficult the group is finding it to contact their anxiety. Accepting this but commenting on the manic behaviour would be the way of doing this.

This is another therapist who clearly regards acting out of this kind as a relatively benign and self-limiting phenomenon. She is therefore able to take the position that the eating and drinking can continue and the group will begin to question what they are doing while they do it.

The author of this chapter was actually a member of the 'party' group and recalls that the group had a culture of insidious acting out which was generally so innocent-looking as to continue unquestioned. It seemed that this was destructive of the analytic process and thereby of each member's therapy. On the actual night of the 'party' the group were all far too busy enjoying mince-pies and wine to give any consideration to deeper matters.

On the other hand when this self-same scenario was role played, on an introductory course in group analysis, a few weeks before Christmas (without any attempt at giving specific characters to individuals), an almighty row broke out in the group with a very fruitful exploration of issues and the uncovering of much grief. The actors got into role very naturally, and it emerged that the father of one member of this group, which was trying to have a party, was very seriously ill in hospital.

NOTES

1 Acting out occurs when unconscious impulses stirred up during therapy are enacted, usually either in symbolic form or by displacement of feelings from the therapist onto an outside person. Acting in occurs when the same process occurs within the limits of the session when the patient is actually with his or her therapist. A patient may wish that his or her therapist would feed him or her more. This wish might then be expressed in coded action by bringing a drink or bar of chocolate into the session.
2 The last supper.
3 S.H. Foulkes (1973) drew our attention to a hypothetical network of communication which is built up over time in a therapy group. He called this the group matrix. He also indicated that each member of the group would bring a personal matrix to the group and share with most of the other members a cultural matrix. At the deepest level, each member also shares with the whole of mankind the *foundation matrix*. This is an idea parallel to Carl Jung's *collective unconscious*.

Chapter 8

Threatened premature termination of therapy

Jeff Roberts

SITUATION 6

A single woman in her thirties, who has been in the group for a year, announces that she is going to leave in four weeks' time – the notice period asked for in the initial guidelines given to members. Although she has gained in confidence during the year, the timing seems premature as there are areas of difficulty which have only begun to be explored in the group – in particular her difficulty in dealing with her own and others' aggressive feelings in the group. When asked by other members about her reasons for leaving, her answers are vague – she does not feel she can get what she wants in this particular group. When pressed further she says she does not really understand it herself. It is now the last of the four sessions of the notice period and it is not clear whether she still intends to leave or has changed her mind.

THE THERAPIST'S TASK AND PROBLEMS

The threat of a premature departure is a relatively common event in the life of a group. The management of this by the conductor requires initially that he or she makes a number of judgements about the statement of a desire to leave:

1. Is it a necessary expression of ambivalence in the form of a fantasy about leaving?

During the course of a long period of group therapy, most members in one way or another speculate about leaving. Some censor this speculation, others let it surface as speculation, while others are more concrete and put it forward in the form of a statement of intent. It is always important to recognise the concrete speculator, because a concrete response to the speculation could lead to a hardening of intent and a totally unnecessary departure.

2. Is it an attempt to resolve a conflict about whether to leave or not, with the help of the group, putting the matter high on the agenda by overstating the level of intent?

In a not too similar way to the concrete speculator, some people are not able to tackle and resolve a conflict in an abstract fashion. A discussion about whether to leave or not can only be achieved as a kind of verbal 'acting out', in which it actually appears that they have a true desire to leave. Again it is important to recognise that this patient is actually offering something up for discussion, not actually making plans.

3. Is it actually a clear statement of intent?

Sometimes a firm intention is offered, as may have happened with the above situation, in such a way that it is either not taken seriously or the group recognise its genuineness but for reasons of their own would prefer not to open up reasons and in a basic assumption[1] (see Chapter 11) kind of behaviour are choosing to ignore both the impending reality of the loss of a member and the fact that the group has a set of mutually agreed ground rules.

4. Is it a ploy: an attempt to evoke interest, gain attention or set up a popularity poll? In this event the member may be seeking something from the conductor, a specific member or members of the group or the whole group.

Self-esteem management is almost universally difficult. Few human beings escape from episodes of either undervaluing or overvaluing themselves. Moreover this is despite the extraordinary lengths to which many people will go to enable themselves to feel worth something. Many of those who fade away and die within a year of retirement have probably, whatever external appearances suggested, been fighting a lifelong battle with low self-esteem. In group therapy, some patients get into difficulties unless regularly acknowledged and appreciated by the group or its conductor. Others seem to require steadily increasing quantities of acknowledgement or appreciation. The announcement of a decision to leave may be the opening gambit of a member with a current self-esteem problem in the group or the continuation of a series of such moves.

5. Is it perhaps an attempt to seek some form of rescue from difficulties in the group from other members of the group or the conductor?

For some people life has become a series of small or large disasters from which rescue is anticipated. The permutations on this scenario are legion. In one the rescuer never arrives and the victim becomes further and further embedded in unresolvable real and imagined difficulties, in another the rescuer always comes and the rescued person gets considerable gratification from the process. In the group situation there is an opportunity to repeat disabling behavioural patterns of this kind and to subject them in the group to an analytic process.

6. Is it an expression of feelings about the group on behalf of the group as a whole?

In the group situation it is not uncommon for the risk-taking member to become the voice of the group. If what is said strongly is not contradicted by other members then it can be assumed that the group as a whole agrees with it. However unpalatable to the conductor this statement is, he or she would do well to attend to it.

7. Is it a threat in the form of: 'If things don't change around here I intend to leave'?

This kind of statement is more or less self-explanatory. It remains for the group and conductor to evaluate whether the implied commands about the group have validity.

The conductor can start to develop hypotheses about the decision to leave the moment it is announced and thereafter will be able to intervene in ways which hopefully would make the underlying motivation increasingly clear. In an effective and mature group-analytic group he or she would be entitled to expect the group to do a lot of this work. Indeed if he or she did too much the group would be increasingly disabled and infantilised. The conductor who manages self-esteem in his or her groups through making many or too clever interventions has for all purposes abandoned Foulkes' maxim that group analysis is 'ego training in action'. The more the conductor exercises his or her ego the less the group members will need to exercise theirs.

If, after giving due consideration to what lies behind a statement of intending to leave, a member abides by this decision to leave, the conductor will wish to evaluate whether this threatened premature departure is mistaken or a recognition from the departee that he or she has come as far as he or she can in the group. Thus the person may be demonstrating an underlying unchangeable rigidity, capacity for psychosis or fear of opening an unbearable wound. In these circumstances it is important not to confront the leaver with his or her real reason for departure but to allow a dignified exit.

Another consideration is that the patient who is indicating his or her intention to leave may feel that he or she has been wounded or otherwise badly treated by the conductor or another member of the group and yet be unable to confront this directly in the group.

Recently one member of a group of the author's (JR), who was giving consideration to leaving, took offence when his therapist suggested that if he did he would have behaved in the group like a butterfly. He used this as the final example of the fact that JR did not understand him at all, which made it impossible for him to stay in the group.

There will also be a number of patients who have a history of difficulties in close relationships, and who might have been better placed in individual therapy either as preparation for joining a group or as an alternative. Such people will often begin to experience a desire to leave when the group goes through phases of increasing intimacy.

A further motivation for leaving in people with long-standing problems in relationships, marked by anticipation of rejection, is a tendency to break off from promising relationships rather than face the inevitable rejection at the hands of the other person or people.

Finally it is important to consider one of the most powerful forces behind irrational and vigorously rationalised departure from the group, namely mirroring. In Chapter 11 of this book it is suggested that particular kinds of response to the group as mirror may be experienced as *peculiarly aversive*. These are likely to be when a member sees in the mirror of the group aspects of the truth about him or herself which he or she either never wishes to know or is currently not ready to know. It is on these occasions that a desire to leave the group is most likely to become overwhelming (see intervention number 6).

THE CONDUCTOR'S ROLE

The conductor's job is to ensure, as far as is possible, that the group and the potentially departing member understand why he or she is (thinking of) leaving the group. In most cases, it is best if the group and the departing member understand the meaning behind the statement of intention to leave and the potential behaviour, i.e. departure from the group, before a final decision is made. Understanding the authentic reason is important both before and after the departure.

In the instance recounted in this chapter's situation it is clear that the woman who intends to leave does not understand her reasons but is experiencing a strong, almost irresistible, compulsion to escape from the group. The conductor has, one hopes, constantly worked to promote understanding but has so far met steadfast resistance. There are few clues as to the potential departee's true motivation although it is noted that she has problems with her own and others' aggression. How true. The whole business of avoiding discussion of the decision to leave up to the last moment is undoubtedly a collusive avoidance of aggression in the group and her sudden unexplained departure is in itself an extremely aggressive act directed at the group and its conductor. If all of this could be surfaced in the group and a more free expression of aggression found by all the members, including the conductor, the leaving would be more honest and probably no longer necessary.

It is important in this instance, as on all occasions where some form of acting out is beginning to occur or is anticipated, that the conductor does his best to maintain an analytic process and reinforce boundaries, without his or her interventions crystallising intent and making unwanted departure more likely. At the same time, the conductor does well if he or she can avoid retaining in the group someone who would ultimately be better leaving.

SELECTED INTERVENTIONS

(F) 'Perhaps you feel uncertain about leaving the group and there are things you would like to understand better. Maybe you'd like to stay on so you can do this.' (1)

Therapist notes – *To allow her to stay if she has changed her mind and to address the feelings of not understanding her own motivation.*

This conductor has addressed the individual and seems in a way to be playing for time. He or she is not addressing the fact that the intention to leave has not been talked about in the intervening period. He or she is choosing not to involve the group and is apparently not setting out to hear from the potential departee where she has got to in the intervening period.

(F) 'We all want you to stay but there seems to be a fear of asking you if you will be doing so.' (2)

Therapist notes – *Allow members to express their needs and sense of impending loss, guilt, etc. Allow woman space for a confident decision.*

This conductor speaks for the group without necessarily knowing what they want!

(M) 'If you were to stay longer in the group, might you get angry with us for not providing what you want?'
    If she says 'Yes', I'll say, 'Go on, what would happen then?'
    If she says 'No, I don't think so', I'll say, 'Why not? – how much deprivation does it take before you get mad?' (3)

Therapist notes – *I think I'm trying to put two questions together in a way that gives either leaving or staying a new significance for her, she'll create that significance for herself in trying to answer my question.*

The therapist here is making the assumption that the decision to leave is based on a failure to get what one wants! In many premature departures this may well be the case, although at the same time this may cover up feelings about other types of events in the group, such as angry encounters with other members and the painful experiences which can go along with reappraisals of oneself, viewed afresh in the mirror(s) provided by the group. *Mirror, mirror on the wall who is the fairest of us all!* I am not sure whether a partial interpretation of anger at the group or the conductor will be sufficient to turn the tide. Indeed there are some departures from a group which are unstoppable and which are as inevitable as the flight of a loosened champagne cork.

(M) If the group did not address the ambiguity, fairly early in the session, I would address it myself.

'It seems we don't know whether you are leaving or not and that is preventing the group from working with their feelings and your feelings about leaving.' (4)

Therapist notes – *In a mature group I usually take a neutral position to patients who plan to leave, leaving it to the group to confront the possible defensiveness of the move. I might point up areas of work still to be done some time but seek to avoid putting pressure on someone to stay in the group. I would prefer to risk someone leaving who should stay to someone leaving at loggerheads with me over their going – it feels to me the latter puts at risk the 'after therapy', the ongoing maturation of the experience gained in the group.*

The group's failure to grasp the nettle of ambiguity and possible conflict is firmly addressed by this conductor, who also hopes that the mature group will tackle the issue of the nature of the decision to leave themselves. On the face of it avoidance of conflict with the departing member is an excellent example of therapeutic tact and forward thinking. One may wonder, however, if the group which is unable to grasp the nettle in the first place and which is able to deny an impending departure for four weeks *is* in a sufficient state of maturity to discuss seriously the appropriateness of the decision. Is this conductor sheltering behind the group and avoiding having to take a position and work with the group and potential departee to become as clear as possible about the real reason for the decision to leave? The real reason may moreover be concealed behind all kinds of rationalisation and subterfuge. The task of the therapist in promoting an honest exchange can become very difficult in this kind of situation, particularly if other members of the group collude with the rationalisations in order to be sure of an easy exit for themselves when their time comes. As a general rule of thumb the more a cast-iron case is offered, particularly if it consists of multiple reasons, the more one can be sure that the real reason is being withheld.

(M) 'I am not clear whether this is your last group or not. Somehow we need to make a decision because we all need to say goodbye if you are leaving. If you wish to stay on then the place is still available because I have not yet spoken to any prospective new member.' (5)

Therapist notes – *Obviously a lot of work COULD be done on what she is doing. However if this is the last group for her then the time is incorrect to attempt work. I think it is more important to be businesslike with her options – stay or leave. If she leaves then I would wish her to leave with our good wishes for the future – possibly in other therapy in the future too.*

This therapist has identified maintenance issues and has also wanted to avoid anything happening in the potential departee's last session which might lead to conflict or unpleasantness. This seems entirely reasonable but it carries a risk of being experienced as colluding with the group's wish to allow this kind of acting out to go by without remark.

(F) 'I think I understand something of your difficulty. It is painful to continue to face the possibility of meeting or dealing with aggressive feelings (yours and other people's) and perhaps deep down this alarms you more than you are aware. Perhaps you are afraid too of how the group would react. Actually it's at these most painful points that you can gain most if you stick it out and work through it. One of my groups calls this the "pain point", it is such a critical time; it needs a lot of courage to stay with it, but I believe you have the courage and could manage it – that is, if you want to.' (6)

Therapist notes – *I would then hope to lead the patient to telling about the part of her that wants to fight and the part of her that doesn't want to stay in the group. If there were previous group situations comparable, I would refer to them and hope (by non-verbal cues to others if necessary) to bring in the thoughts of other group members. The rest of the process would have to stand the test of the patient's motivation.* The negative transference if this is identifiable should be interpreted *(as to the conductor, individual members and the group as a whole).*

This is a very concerned, full and tightly argued intervention which attempts to identify precisely the experience of the group member and appeals to the motivation of the member to continue in therapy, even though the whole business has now started to be far more difficult and painful than originally anticipated. The therapist is, whilst attempting to point out the deeper unconscious motivation behind the decision to leave, also appealing to the 'treatment alliance'.[2] The 'treatment alliance' is the original agreement between therapist and the 'conflict-free ego' of his or her patient, that they will work together to understand and resolve neurotic conflicts through a therapeutic process such as involvement in a therapy group. This initial agreement includes an expectation that treatment will last a given amount of time, such as two years, and be terminable by mutual agreement and only after careful discussion. However, as the patient becomes caught up in the group process and both negative and positive transferences develop, so the amount of his or her conflict-free ego tends to diminish. The patient tends then to forget initial agreements and the therapeutic alliance founders, sometimes irretrievably. This intervention exemplifies the way in which the group members' participation in therapy is always balanced on a tightrope of how much insight they can tolerate without needing to find ways of avoiding too much intolerable truth about themselves, other people and the world that they live in. The intervention offered here is extremely caring and holding, offering a good chance that the patient or client who hears it will be encouraged to venture that much further along a painful journey.

(M) 'Well, are you going to leave? Or going to stay?' (I would hope the group members said this.) 'Aren't we all avoiding the issue, pussy-footing around? We haven't pushed you to decide and you're frightened to stick your neck out. Isn't this the real problem that both you need to stay in the group for, and the group needs to face up to?' (7)

Therapist notes – With all this meandering she'll go and the group will be able to avoid the issue yet longer. The tone of the comment has to challenge the issues which are being avoided – particularly at this time avoidance of the anger at leaving and being left.

This conductor also identifies courage or a lack of it as a contributor to the development of this situation. This seems a very reasonable hypothesis and it seems likely that every member of the group, including the conductor, has lacked courage in allowing matters to come to a head at the last possible moment. This is typical of much human behaviour in which risky or potentially painful experiences are postponed repeatedly, until a point is reached when further postponement is not possible. Our previous conductor has pinpointed the problems of a lack of courage in the departing member and chooses a thorough and understanding approach to this. Her belief is that gentle understanding will strengthen the resolve of her wavering member. The conductor currently being considered is far more confronting and punitive and is hoping that resolve will be strengthened by highlighting and challenging the weakness which is apparent. It would be hard to state definitively that one or other method was likely to be more effective. Every conductor will develop his or her own style (see Chapter 1).

(M) 'Hasten not in the day of the clouds' is an old adage that seems applicable here. (8)

Therapist notes – If she wishes to leave she has the right. By my interpretation I am leaving the door of possibility open without pointing the way to it.

Metaphorical statements can resonate deeply in a person's psyche, as Cox (Cox and Thielgaard 1987) points out, usually without disturbing the surface. Thus, where the dream is the 'Royal Road' whereby the unconscious finds outward expression, so metaphor provides a way in. My initial problem with this intervention is that I don't understand it. If it resonates deeply, then no matter; moreover my struggle to understand this communication is likely to lead to a useful gain in my ability to understand emotionally charged situations and the language with which they can be managed. If the group will struggle with this concentrated communication the crisis may be successfully dealt with and maturation occur all round. Metaphorical approaches can, however, evoke strong, angry resistance from some group members, and if the group is in a resistant mood, as this one appears to be, instead of penetrating deeply this statement may flow away 'like water off a duck's back'.

NOTES

1 One of the hallmarks of a basic assumption mode of functioning is an apparent unawareness on the part of a group of all of the constraints of time and place and the 'rules which determine the ways in which time and place are used'.
2 Sandler, Dare and Holder (1973) give a lucid and helpful exposition of the complexities of the therapeutic relationship in Chapters 3, 4, 5 and 6 of their book *The Patient and the Analyist.*

Chapter 9

Disillusionment with therapy

Yiannis Arzoumanides

SITUATION 7

This group has been meeting for over two years and their early idealisations of the group and its conductor have been replaced by varying styles and degrees of disillusionment. Today the group chorus is concerned with the uselessness of psychotherapy. You do not respond and they repeat the theme more loudly until one by one they fall silent. The silence has lasted for fourteen minutes and there are three minutes to go before the end of the group.

THE THERAPIST'S TASK AND PROBLEMS

The above vignette is taken from a group that goes through a phase of disillusionment. The group's reaction to the non-responsive facilitator, who lets the silence develop, raises a number of issues.

This is an important phase in the group's life. It seems that the group goes through a transitional period during which some of its members or the group as a whole move from dependence to independence (Winnicott, 1982; Klein, 1984) and thus go through a period of ambivalence (Klein, 1984). The members of the group are not sure whether group therapy is beneficial to them; whether the group therapist is a competent one or, to use Winnicott's term, a good enough parent; or whether or not they like the other group members. Eventually there comes a point where the 'magic' of psychotherapy is not there any more. Then they question the value of group psychotherapy as a whole and later on they might find themselves faced with the dilemma of whether to continue therapy or not.

It can be argued that the group as a whole and its members are in a phase of being in touch with what Klein has called a bad object, towards which they express their anger and frustration by attacking it. Much of the hatred against parts of the self is now directed towards the mother, and specifically 'the mother's breast' (Klein, 1984). The mother here can be the group, the psychotherapy or the conductor and therefore the group, psychotherapy or the conductor is useless.

Timing of the intervention is of major importance and careful consideration should be given to whether to intervene early or let the silence develop and end the session without any intervention. If the therapist intervenes early, the possible aim is to facilitate communication within the group and thus help the group members to explore their disillusionment with group psychotherapy and additionally explore further the symbolic meaning of this disillusionment. Here the conductor gives them the indirect message that they can depend on him or her for help and solutions. If he or she lets the silence develop then the possible aim is to allow the group members to go through the tension and decide for themselves the next move, thus giving them responsibility and freedom.

Of course, the decision to follow the one or the other course depends on the individual therapist and his or her training, the structure of the group and the group's developmental stage. The factors that should be taken into account include:

1. Has the group been meeting long enough that it can be considered an established and cohesive one?

2. The disillusionment might be nothing more than a necessary stage in the group's development as well as that of its individual members, in which it is a means of expressing negative transference.

3. It is also possible that the group is going through a normal stage in its development in which the patients realise that they also have power. In this stage the members of the group realise that, after all, help comes from the combined efforts of the group and the individual himself or herself.

With regard to the last point, it can be argued that group development follows a similar course to that of the child who realises that he/she too has power and is able to influence with his/her actions the world around him/her and do things for himself/herself. From a state of complete dependency, or as Balint (1968) calls it 'total togetherness', the group and each of its members, like the child, is moving towards independence and in doing so gets in touch consciously or unconsciously with primitive levels of development. Like the nurturing mother, the group conductor is not there any more. Depending on the ego strength of the group and its members, this realisation brings a number of conflicting feelings such as depression, anger and excitement to different degrees.

This particular group is primarily concerned with the 'uselessness of psychotherapy', indicating that they are not prepared to accept responsibility for their condition and stage of development. It is in this stage that the child, or group, has to 'kill the father' in order to be free of him before being able to re-establish a relationship in an adult way.

The group has tried to engage the therapist but help has not come from him/her. So after repeated attempts – clear indications of their dependency – they fall into silence, thus separating from each other and expressing their negative transference towards the therapist (Yalom, 1985). This expression of negative transference, by taking the view that 'The group is not good for me; I should look somewhere else', is analogous to the child's phase of denying one or both parents. In the here and now of the group situation, such feelings may be re-experienced and worked through in the relationship with the therapist. In other words, the group may be seen to be in touch with its unconscious struggle with authority and need for independence. This is expressed by denying all good in group psychotherapy, in the therapist and thus indirectly in everyone who was and still is in authority.

Disillusionment can be seen as having both negative and positive facets depending on the individual's ego strength. If, for example, the person is fragile, with low self-esteem and a weak ego, it can be experienced as helplessness, which may lead to panic and desperation. On the other hand, disillusionment can be experienced as elation, associated with the feeling that 'I am free and able to make my own decisions'. This attitude eventually will bring the person to a point of self-actualisation and the ability to say 'this is what I want to do in my life', and then to do it.

SELECTED INTERVENTIONS

The interventions may be classified into groups according to:

  i) their timing;

  ii) their content.

The first group of therapists was prepared to remain silent to the end, making no comment at all, merely indicating the end of the session. Their responses to the questionnaire included:

(M) I would make no comment. (1)

Therapist notes – *The group appears cohesive; usually after the phase of idealisation the group will become more realistic. Here, probably expressing depression and aggression in the next group.*

(M) Let the silence go on till the end. (2)

Therapist notes – *but would come back to it in the subsequent session if this feeling is not dealt with by the group. I would not be so worried about a 14-minute silence in a two-year-old group unless there was a very fragile patient in it.*

(M) I would remain silent, I would maintain a blank screen! (3)

Therapist notes – *Important not to be coerced into providing salvation. Because group is well established the anxieties from silence should be contained. Position would be different if individual members were not presently robust.*

(M) None. (4)

Therapist notes – *After two years a group can need and tolerate longer silences and space. Something said in the last minutes by a conductor may seem to undermine.*

(M) If this group is fairly cohesive by now I might just leave the silence and say nothing. (5)

Therapist notes – *I'd see this disenchantment as an important group phase and event for the group to work through.*

(M) I would say absolutely nothing. (6)

Therapist notes – *I would not want to rescue them from their despair of having lost their ideal. Once they are allowed to hit bottom without rescue they should then come up again. My silence also emphasises my 'uselessness' but it also implies that I don't need defending.*

These therapists are determined to make no detailed comment. Their decision is based on their feelings that (a) the group after two years is cohesive and well established; (b) there is no member at risk or fragile; and (c) the group is moving from a phase of idealisation to a more realistic one. Emphasis was given to the fact that in a well-established group silences should be contained.

The second group of therapists remain silent until just before the end of the group, when they make a short intervention. For example:

(M) Say nothing until the end – then quietly, 'It's time'. (7)

Therapist notes – *Group is a long-standing one, and I'm guessing they have the stamina to leave this one dangling till next week. My remark shows I'm still alive.*

(M) At this point I would continue to sit quietly and in the last minute say 'I'll see you all next week'. (8)

Therapist notes – *I'd be unhappy with this group – but it has happened like this. If I had no useful interventions to make till now then I have to trust in the structure of the group to continue the analytic process.*

(F) I think I should break the silence before departure with a comment such as 'It feels so sad when high hopes are dashed and I begin to wonder if the group will be here next week at all'. (9)

Therapist notes – *Naming the fear. Attention to the anger would be difficult unless someone gave an angry response in which case it would be validated and accepted. Their problem would seem to be where to place the blame and they are in a mourning mode for loss of the idealised group (and the idealised therapist).*

(M) Perhaps it might help to share what is going through my mind. I feel very uncomfortable and that something in the mood of the group is blocking things, perhaps next week we could begin by trying to talk it out. (10)

Therapist notes – *I shouldn't have let it go on this long; however, I feel immobilised by the disappointment and hostility of the group. However if they can voice it this block might be removed, and their dependence on me resolved. It is too late today however, but I had to say something to instil a bit of momentum and optimism before we go.*

These therapists, while prepared to tolerate a lengthy silence, wish to leave the group with an indication of their continued involvement in it. In some cases, this consists of an acknowledgement of the feelings which the group is experiencing, some pointers as to what may be underlying these and the anticipation that the group's impasse will be overcome.

A third group of therapists would make a more detailed intervention. Some of these therapists indicated that they would have preferred to intervene much earlier. While expressing concern as to whether they should have left the silence to go on for so long, they gave an 'if I had' response to the situation. For example:

(F) I don't think I would have let such a long silence develop leaving only three minutes to finish. However if I had: 'You all are obviously feeling very let down by me today that I have not made things better for you. Your anger at me I think has blocked off the fact that each of you has isolated yourself from one another, making you believe that help can only come from one source, that is me. You have forgotten that you are the group. (11)

(F) 'It seems that group members are pretty disenchanted with this group' – (? and with each other including me). I wouldn't let this silence in this situation go on fourteen minutes. What for? (12)

Therapist notes – *1) Try to get into this group. 2) Try to get a lever on the discontentment – What is it about? What do they want? Are they discontented with me, or is there something going on between group members that hasn't come out into the open yet?*

(F) Here in New Zealand, YOU DON'T have fourteen-minute silences. It's just not part of our culture; I've never had any group could stand that kind of anxiety. After three to four minutes, I'd try to get them going by asking, very non-specifically, what this silence said about what we'd just been discussing. And I'd look directly at various members, soliciting their responses, if silence continues, comment on their need for me to 'take control' and give them something, some 'answer', some solution.

Therapist notes – *(Maybe after two years they'd be able to come back and get on with it next week.) It would be necessary, I feel, to offer something 'positive' – probably along the lines of having grown beyond looking to the omnipotent therapist, but finding it in the group, when we use it as a group.*

The more detailed group of interventions may be classified in terms of their content. Some therapists focus on the aggression towards them which they regard as underlying the group's disillusionment with therapy. They adopt different ways of addressing this aggression. Some make a direct interpretation that the silence may be a form of aggression directed towards the therapist; some just indicate that the group is experiencing anger, thus bringing it into the open and facilitating communication; and others let the group deal with these feelings according to its developmental stage. For example:

(F) I would, I hope, have been able to take an emotional 'temperature reading' of the silence – and I would hope to have been able to identify it as angry, depressed, contemplative or whatever – probably anger and depression. I would then, before the end of the session, comment – e.g.: 'There seems to be too much anger, disappointment and depression to speak. The feeling I've let you down is very intense – it's like facing a useless parent, all the worse because of the earlier trust and feeling of promise. I think some of you are torn between wanting to cry and wanting to kick me in the teeth/bash me/destroy me' (depending on the group level, language and culture). I'd then wait for the response. If there was no verbal response, I would leave the silence to continue until the end of the session. I would observe, but not comment on, non-verbal responses. (13)

(M) 'The group appears angry. You seem to know how you have got where you are, and are now faced with the responsibility of change.' (14)

Therapist notes – *The shadow side of idealisation is anger, if not violence. This silence feels like repressed aggression. My comment was designed to evoke the repressed anger, (the useless bastard!) Then the group can release its energy, fear, frustration . . .*

(M) I might say, with a twinkle, 'So where do we go from here?' (15)

Therapist notes – *I want to signal that what they are experiencing is appropriate and that there is a way forward and that I am expecting them to find it. I would expect my remark to provoke a more open expression of anger, if not within three minutes then next session.*

(M) 'We'll have to finish in a few minutes. What has been happening in the silence?' If no reply: 'I was thinking that the group is very united at the moment in writing me off as useless. I wonder how that makes you feel?' (16)

Therapist notes – *Rather than leave it as though I was engaged in a skulking battle, I would invite them to explore the meaning of the silence and the feelings and fantasies it expresses and provokes. By acknowledging the anger at me I would demonstrate that I was not afraid of it.*

(F) (I would not let silence continue for fourteen minutes at the end of the group.) 'I am concerned about what is happening in the group. A great deal of needy feelings have been expressed in the past and now there is a strong sense of disappointment and hurt and anger. I am seriously afraid that we are not going to be able to work on this because of the strength of these feelings. There isn't much time today but we must come back to it next week.' (17)

Therapist notes – *The disengagement seems to me a way of dealing with what feels like intolerable, irresolvable feelings. Therapist should demonstrate his continuing involvement and engagement. Next week I should want to look at whether this is habitual with disappointment. If necessary by direct approach. . .*

(F) 'It sounds as if the group is angry with me. I wonder why you feel you cannot talk about it.' I suppose that if I were more strong minded, I might have left the silence to continue, with the intention of using the experience in the next session, but I probably would have made the above comment in an attempt to 'hold' members in anticipation of an excessive carry over of anxiety. (18)

Other therapists focus primarily on the depression which the group is experiencing. Some are prepared to acknowledge this depression and to help the group out of it, while others feel that the group is strong enough to deal on its own with this depressive position, thus facilitating growth. These therapists' responses included:

(M) (a) If the group seemed cohesive and none of the individuals at risk from my non-intervention I might well say nothing. (b) Otherwise I would acknowledge their depression with 'We seem very very depressed' in a matter-of-fact tone of voice. (19)

Therapist notes – *If group and individuals are strong enough there seems benefit in struggling with this depressive position without therapist assistance . . .*

(M) 'There seems to be some depression around: you seem to be disappointed in group psychotherapy and perhaps worried that that's all you're going to get out of it.' (20)

Therapist notes – *Personally, I find it difficult to end the group session with such a feeling of rejection. In my experience the group response to the above comments is a 'manic' one, although it would be too late to make use of it.*

Yet other therapists pointed out that responsibility is what members of the group should explore, and that especially they should take responsibility for their decisions and actions in the particular session and stage that they are in. Again, some preferred to use an interpretation while others felt that it was not appropriate at this point in time. For example:

(F) 'You are determined to show me that I am useless here. There seems to be a wish to deny that anything can help! It's far more comfortable to hide behind the idea that nothing is any good rather than to tackle the responsibility of overcoming whatever is blocking you. . . . See you all next week.' (21)

Therapist notes – *A mild challenge to their own responsibilities seems indicated. I am not sure I would leave it until the last three minutes of the session.*

(F) 'It seems as if the way the group has ended today marks the beginning of a change in its life – as if there is a consensus amongst you to accept the necessity, reluctantly, for personal responsibility in the face of disillusion and sadness. That one day the group, and ultimately life itself, will end.' (22)

(F) 'It seems that this group has reached the end of a phase and is ready for the next one, which is to carry on without illusions and to accept reality. This puts of course more responsibility on you.' (23)

Therapist notes – *It is important to see disillusionment as a sign of growth and development rather than failure of the group.*

For some of these therapists, the situation which the group faced, and for which it was encouraged to take responsibility, was seen as no less than a reflection of the existential paradox of life itself. They chose anecdotal interventions as the most appropriate means of drawing the group's attention to these existential concerns:

(M) 'A mother had twin sons, one an optimist and the other a pessimist. To the former she gave a ton of dung, to the latter a gold watch. On seeing his present, the optimist explained "With all this dung, there must be a horse somewhere". The latter said (on seeing the watch) "I'm sure it will be stolen!" ' (24)

Therapist notes – *A group in such a situation is faced with the essential* paradox *of life itself. I never try to solve this paradox either for myself or them – I just allow them to* face *it clearly.*

(M) 'There's an old American therapist who says the best way to avoid psycho-therapy is to have regular meetings with a psychotherapist!' (25)

Therapist notes – *I'm using my own free association. I'm saying something that is difficult to respond to directly but challenges them to think about (or rethink) what they're saying in a different way. There's an implication in my comment that it's not what you get but what you do with it. It's an existential sort of frame.*

We have seen that there was a wide spectrum of responses to this situation. Some therapists were determined not to comment on the silence but to leave the group to deal with it in the best way it could, thus providing the group with an opportunity to tackle its depressive position, to develop its sense of responsibility and to move towards reality. Some opted for the other end of the spectrum, expressing concern as to whether it was appropriate to let the silence go on for so long. Most of them would have wanted to intervene much earlier, and found a fourteen-minute silence to be unproductive.

As our sample of interventions has indicated, silences in the group and the timing of the therapist's response are topics of vital importance in therapy, requiring special attention.

Chapter 10

A threat of physical violence

Yiannis Arzoumanides and Jeff Roberts

SITUATION 8

A borderline patient has been in an established group for eighteen months. She seems unable to take in any group support and her moods change quite quickly. In this session four of the six members are present. The patient is unable to get her feelings out about the therapist. Near the end of the group she erupts in violence and, producing a razor blade, she threatens to 'carve you up'. Two members flee in panic.[1]

THE THERAPIST'S TASK AND PROBLEMS

This is a major crisis in the life of the group. The therapist here must quickly establish his or her priorities and course of action. He or she should decide whether to deal first with the group as a whole, those members who have left the room or the borderline patient, and in what way. Should one try to stop members of the group leaving the room? Should one deal with the physical threat in a physical way or should one attempt to contain the situation within a verbal framework? It might indeed seem almost laughable to attempt to deal with such a physically threatening situation in an interpretative fashion. 'Typical unworldly analyst', might be the reader's response. Yet this threat may only be theatre and even now a long way from being carried out. The borderline patient is often not able to distinguish reality and fantasy, so that if the conductor is able to hold onto his or her belief that the patient is still having fantasies of a carve up, in reality it may never happen. A precipitate attempt at disarming may make the violence all too real!

One of the tasks of the therapist is to protect members of a group from harming themselves and each other. Thoughts will probably race through the therapist's mind. How reliable are these thoughts? Unexpected threats of violence are not conducive in most people to cool, orderly thinking. In the first few moments after the threat the therapist will experience an impulse to react. A large bolus of adrenaline will undoubtedly have our therapist experiencing butterflies in the stomach, shaking hands, racing pulse and weak knees. He or she will have a strong inclination to 'fight' or 'fly'. This would manifest itself in either a strong desire to follow the fleeing duo or to take up the challenge and give the miscreant as good as offered! Only by resisting these impulses can the therapist hope to regain access to his or her therapeutic self and find a more reflective and creative response. In the heat of the moment will there be time for this? If the therapist has past experience of encounters with impulse-driven behaviour and has digested this experience there probably will be time. This desirable outcome is more likely if the therapist can indicate that he or she has his or her own fear and rage under control and that he or she genuinely desires a dialogue. The therapist must attempt to interpose a delay between the impulse and the action in both him or herself and the client. This allows time for thinking. Second thoughts in such a situation are usually better than the instantaneous impulse-contaminated first thoughts. If it proves impossible to interpose a delay then the battle is lost and the therapeutic framework is destroyed.

It will become clear in the second part of this chapter that some of the therapists have acted out themselves in response to this particular patient's disequilibrium.

One of the therapist's initial second thoughts is likely to be 'How can I help this group hold together and in safety?' The therapist needs to defuse the situation without losing an opportunity to use it therapeutically since acting out is a dramatic form of communication and often expresses hidden agendas that have been kept under control for lengthy periods of time.

A method of defusing acting out is by interpreting well before and at the right moment the conflict or the fantasy which is likely to be acted out. Correct timing is crucial for success of an intervention that can prevent destructive acting out from taking place. It is also of considerable importance in preventive terms to be closely in touch with the ongoing process of one's borderline patients and to work hard with them to maintain a mutually agreed reality, with an avoidance of extremes of transference distortion. These preventive measures can facilitate considerable change within a carefully maintained therapeutic alliance. If this is not possible or has not been achieved, then the therapist has to decide on the best way to deal with acting out when it occurs.

The therapist must ultimately ask, 'What is the meaning of this blind behaviour?' Thus, as was originally stated by Freud, those who cannot remember and understand their past will blindly repeat it. When patients act out, it is necessary to pay close attention to the messages implicit in this behaviour, so that psychopathology is revealed and attempts made to help the actors change – through understanding associations to the past enfolded within their compulsive activity. However, one must take cognisance of the goals and the patient's readiness to accept and use that which is uncovered. It has been argued that acting out is irrational behaviour, often destructive, which, if not analysed, understood and worked through before or after it occurs, has very small therapeutic effect. The therapist involved in this scenario must explore the underlying mental content that motivated the patient to produce a razor and threaten violence. Also important is the understanding of the symbolic elements of acting out. The ultimate goal is to help the client to become aware of what she is doing, why she is doing it and how to free herself from doing it again.

A therapist needs to have explored in his or her thinking the advantages and disadvantages of acting out and how it can be used therapeutically or its occurrence minimised. Having considered this, the therapist will be prepared to deal with it when it happens, especially when it happens in this extreme way.

It has been identified that acting out exists inside and outside the group. Some therapists regard all acting out as destructive and irrational, others argue that it provides the therapist and the group with important insights (Agazarian and Peters, 1981, p. 202) and that it can be used therapeutically. Acting out outside the group may be resistance – a substitute for remembering and coping with the problem within the group. In the razor incident it could be argued that the patient's ability to express her anger in this violent way can be viewed as progress since the action took place in the group rather than outside, where nobody could have challenged the patient's distorted perceptions. Additionally, acting out in a public place might have resulted in harming somebody or herself and then becoming subject to police control and legal sanctions.

In general, therapists do not like destructive behaviour but when it happens they should try to be in control of the incident, not punish for it, and try any possible therapeutic attempt before resorting to prohibition. None the less, feelings are better expressed verbally and early, rather than through action later. Having said that, we should not forget that sometimes, due to the client's history, there is an underlying desire for and need to be controlled, with an implicit awareness that this control is not available internally. Such a client usually feels relief when external control is provided. This form of controlling gives the message that somebody cares, and that he or she is in a safe environment.

It is also essential to take into account the reaction of the other group members and hear what they have to say about the incident. The long-term fate of the 'acting out' patients in the group will depend very much on the group's reaction to them and the way in which the incident is explored and understood. Moreover, the group may have either a strong negative or positive investment in this client since she may have been expressing not only her anger but the group's anger as well.

A final feature of this situation which may be of significance is that it seems to the authors that it is more common for razor blades to be used for the type of delicate self-cutting which rarely leads to death or even serious injury. The act of cutting diminishes tension and gives the patient a visible external wound which can be shown to others quietly and insistently with an underlying communication of 'look what you made me do!' In this case the rage is externalised, a sign of progress of a sort, and in her rage the patient threatens the body of her therapist and opens up the body of the group which 'bleeds' two members.

SELECTED INTERVENTIONS

The experienced therapists were remarkably diverse in their approach to the challenge of this situation. Their primary interventions may be divided up as follows.

Physical restraint.

A verbal response instructing the patient to 'Put the razor blade away'.

A verbal response aimed at interpreting the motivation behind the action.

A verbal response dealing with boundary issues.

An attempt to retrieve those who flew.

These were the main concerns of almost all therapists. Their differences were in the sequence of their responses. Some preferred to respond verbally first and then if necessary physically. Others wanted to stop group members leaving the room and then to deal with the errant client and the issue of acting out, while yet others dealt with the client first and then with the group.

In the following section the interventions are reviewed according to the therapist's first response.

Physical restraint

Some therapists indicated in their intervention an acknowledgement or indeed expectation that the threat would be carried out and were concerned with restraining the client physically should it become necessary. There were various styles of doing this.

(F) If she came towards me I would have to ward her off physically and I hope gently at the same time talking to her. (1)

(M) . . . If she got up and attacked me I would use such force as was necessary to disarm her. (2)

(M) . . . If she's standing – 'SIT DOWN'. If attacking – use my feet to kick her away. (3)

(M) . . . If she attacked I would give her a good right. (4)

(M) A rapid assessment with an immediate readiness to restrain her physically or flee as well calling on other members. (5)

(M) I would address her by name and say quietly 'I believe other members of the group are furious with me too.' But I would be ready, if she began to act on her statement, to overpower and disarm her, calling on the assistance of other members, and then to warn her that any future act of violence would mean she would immediately lose her place in the group. (6)

Therapist notes – *The borderline member often speaks the group's unconscious feelings. Actual violence is intolerable: the threat of it might be worked with.*

(F) (Non-verbally send a lot of signals to other group members!) . . . Ask patient, very quietly, to talk to us about what it's all about. Check out real defensive possibilities – chair or cushions within reach? (7)

Therapist notes – *Key question is, can this be 'dealt with', or is it a complete psychotic break; if so physical restraint will be required for everyone's safety.*

A verbal response instructing the patient to put the razor blade away

(M) Talk loudly: 'Put that away please!' 'I'm not having that here' . . . 'Now what's it all about?' (to the borderline patient). (8)

(M) 'Put the blade away!' (9)

(F) 'Please give me the razor blade.' (10)

(M) 'But you really should put the blade away and try to reach your feelings.' (11)

(F) 'Your anger seems almost unbearable. You must be feeling the group and I haven't helped you at all.' I would then, depending on circumstances, possibly suggest dropping the razor blade on the floor or giving it to me or putting it away. I'd then ask 'Do you want me all to yourself?' And later, 'Do you feel I'm so useless that even if you had me all to yourself it wouldn't be any good?' (12)

Therapist notes – *You'd really have to be involved in the anteceding sessions to make an accurate response – what is required is an accurately empathic statement, incorporating what you know of the patient's feelings. You may, for example, indicate that it is unbearably painful for the patient to sense any closeness developing – it threatens and frightens her, whether from the conductor or other group members.*

(M) 'Your words are enough to make me feel your anger and the razor you can put away.' (13)

Very few of our therapists in fact do not make some attempt to persuade this patient to seek and verbally express her feelings. There is, however, a great variation in the way the threat is to be dealt with. In the above sequence some therapists adopt a non-aggressive and non-authoritarian mode, and appear to be adopting a 'submissive' and non-threatening posture in order to diminish the confrontational nature of the situation. Others seem more to hope that the patient will automatically respond to a command. One has to *be* commanding for this to happen. Others seem to be meeting the aggression with aggression, almost intent on frightening the patient into submission. Finally, the most subtle of therapists incorporate an expectation that the blade will not be used in a more or less interpretative comment like the final example above. The choice of intervention style will be in part a function of the style and character of the therapist but will also inevitably be determined by his or her best attempt at an objective evaluation of the client and her ability to regain control.

A verbal response aimed at interpreting the motivation behind the action

(F) 'I can see how you feel that no-one understands or takes your anger seriously and that you think the only way is to demonstrate it. Please now try to sit and explain to us what you are feeling inside. Sit by me and tell us.' (14)

(M) 'Two members have expressed your fear by leaving. You attack what is given you, rather than taking it in. You are afraid of how much you need now.' (15)

(M) 'I can see that your feelings towards me must be very sharp, very cutting. It is good to get that out in the open. Not everyone can bear it to have feelings about me or the group as lacerating as yours. That is probably why they have gone. But you really should put the blade away and try and reach your feelings.' (16)

(F) 'Your anger seems almost unbearable. You must be feeling the group and I haven't helped you at all.' (17)

(M) 'You must hate me for not offering you support and being interested and caring for the others. You want to carve me out of the group to have me for yourself – and carve me out of yourself so you can be free.' (18)

(F) 'Your act of hostility towards me is perhaps an attempt to break out of isolation and to communicate your frustration and rage – no doubt others in the group can understand this.' (19)

(M) 'You may be disappointed that I have not managed to rid you of your bad feelings and that you're going to go away with them . . .' (20)

(F) 'Perhaps you feel like carving me up because you feel upset and frustrated about not getting what you need from me and the group.' (21)

(M) 'You seem afraid that the group and I are unable to help you, or even understand how desperate and furious you feel at times.' (22)

(F) 'I do not want you to harm me but I can see that you have very strong feelings. Do you think that by "carving me up" I could then give you a piece of myself which you could keep and not have to share with the other members?' (23)

(F) 'You want me to hurt like you do?' (24)

These therapists are in one way or another seeking to access the unexpressed and inexpressible unconscious ideation underlying the behaviour. As discussed above, this kind of primitive behaviour is likely to have at its root a sense of having been wounded during early development by deprivation or trauma visited on the 'victim' by his or her parents. Such wounds are a source of inner pain and a continuing desire for revenge. The bearer of such wounds can gain from being able to articulate this experience in words, thereby no longer being compelled to re-enact the experience in a primitive fashion. The therapists here are attempting in a variety of ways to enable this client's access to these deeply disturbing experiences. In the long run their aim would be to introduce the notion of the healing of wounds and the futility of holding onto a revenge motive throughout one's life.

A verbal response dealing with boundary issues

(M) 'You know that however angry we are physical violence is forbidden in this group' – as authoritatively as possible. (25)

(M) 'OK. You're angry with me, but we use words here. You can too I think' . . . and then to warn her that any future act of violence would mean she would immediately lose her place in the group. (26)

(F) 'In the group we can talk about being angry but I'm not prepared to have any physical attacking here.' (27)

(M) 'You do have the right to be heard and I hope understood here though you mustn't frighten people.' (28)

(F) 'Please put that razor blade away – As I explained to you before your joining this is a TALKING GROUP – can you try to say what you feel in words, then perhaps we will be able to get somewhere with it.' (29)

(M) 'There is to be no violence expressed in this group; either put that razor blade away or get out. Physical violence is something which is not on as it makes the group completely unsafe for therapy.' (30)

(M) Experience of violent borderline patients is that avoiding extremes of fear/anger is calming. I'd be doing my best to re-establish boundaries and control for the patient. If need be I'd have to make a direct statement to that effect. (31)

The loss of boundaries is contrary to the fundamental principles of therapy and extremely alarming to many therapists. Interventions which restore or reaffirm boundaries are reassuring to therapists, who then congratulate themselves on how relieved the patient has been by the boundary maintenance. Often this is the case, but it is surely often also true that the generation of chaos and the indulgence of impulses can be thrilling indeed and the therapist will need to encompass this in his or her intervention.

An attempt to retrieve those who flew

(F) If she came towards me I would have to ward her off physically and I hope gently at the same time talking to her. If I also had the presence of mind I think I would ask one of the remaining members of the group to try and get the other two back. (32)

(F) I would try and get the panicky members to return to the group and say, 'Let's look at this quietly. Why does Y have to express her feelings in this way, what makes it so hard for her just to say how bad she feels? What does it mean to have an outburst threatening violence? [To Y] Who are you really wanting to hurt?' (33)

Therapist notes – *Main point is to keep unperturbed and in control of the group, therefore it's important to get the panicky members back. I may have to keep talking for quite a while to stop the panic; this should also help in taking the sting out of the aggression.*

(F) I stand up and try to prevent the two members leaving (that is if they are still in the room). I ask them to sit down. (34)

The patient is here threatening to cut open the body of the therapist. A most alarming prospect, for the therapist, the other patients and no doubt for the protagonist herself. The bleeding of two members of the group is analogous to the potential bleeding of the therapist, so that a desirable closure of such a situation is the containment of the threat plus a retrieval of those who fled. All has then been contained. Clearly those therapists who give attention to the fleeing members have such an outcome in mind. This approach is to be admired although when a group member gets up to flee he or she is almost always unstoppable. The containment is usually achieved at the following session when the prodigal(s) return(s).

CONCLUDING REMARKS

As far as is possible one should allow and expect the emergence of disturbed feelings, thoughts and behaviour during the course of therapy. One cannot forbid all acting out in the group, as this would be too limiting of the group members' means of expression and would prevent the emergence of some elements of transference which could provide the group with information about each member. However, balanced against this is the need to protect the integrity of the group as a safe therapeutic space and, further, to funnel the expression of rage and despair in the direction of conscious verbalisation, thereby increasing self-awareness and the possibility of conscious control of behaviour and life strategies.

NOTE

1 It is not clear from the account of this situation whether the borderline patient stood up and went towards the therapist or whether she produced the razor whilst sitting and said from her place 'I will carve you up'.

The above description leaves this open to speculation and therefore to different reactions. This ambiguity has probably contributed to the variety of responses, with each of the participants developing a different picture as he or she visualised him or herself in the situation.

Chapter 11

Intervening to establish and maintain a therapeutic environment

Jeff Roberts

The conductor of a therapeutic group is aiming both to offer a therapy to individuals and also to develop a therapeutic environment in his or her group. He or she will therefore need to both look after the individual members and look after the group. The needs of the group at any moment may not always be the same as the needs of the individual, even though in the long term the needs of the individuals will be best served through the development of a therapeutic environment in the group and the development of the group as an instrument of therapy. Most group analysts believe that the adoption of the methods advocated by S.H. Foulkes will result in the development of a benign therapeutic environment and an effective therapeutic group. However, destructive processes can occur in groups that may for short or even long periods render them at best non-therapeutic and at worst harmful. In the following sections consideration is given to the balance of destructive and constructive processes in the group and how the conductor's interventions may influence this.

THE GROUP MATRIX

The idea of the matrix is believed to be one of Foulkes' most important contributions to group-analytic theory. He defined the group matrix on a number of occasions. One of the most accessible of these definitions is as follows:

> The matrix is the hypothetical web of communication and relationship in a given group. It is the common shared ground which ultimately determines the meaning

and significance of all events and upon which all communications verbal and non verbal rest.

(Foulkes, 1964)

With the generation of this idea he provided a means of linking our understanding of human communication in groups with a substantial body of science to do with creation and metamorphosis. In a previous paper Roberts wrote:

> According to the Analytical Psychologists, particularly Neumann (1970), consciousness can be thought of as an (individual) creation that has emerged slowly and painfully out of the collective unconscious over many millennia. Foulkes effectively says the same and in promoting group analysis was, it might be suggested, intimating that it is therapeutic to submerge one's consciousness in a group to struggle to emerge from the group having strengthened and redefined it. Thus the development of consciousness can be closely related to the figure/ground phenomena of perception, and be seen (somewhat simplistically, but accurately) as defining oneself against a background. The group matrix can form such a background, from which a damaged individual (consciousness) may emerge revitalized. This point of view corresponds nicely with other meanings (*Oxford English Dictionary*, 1971) of the word matrix:
>
> 1. Mother, pregnant or otherwise.
> 2. Womb.
> 3. Background substance.
> 4. Mould, in which something is made.
> 5. *Place where something with structure, often alive and perhaps extremely valuable, is held during its formation or transformation.*
>
> (Roberts, 1983)

Roberts suggests that 'the group matrix can be viewed as a context in which a safe and remarkably deep regression may be obtained, with a potential for enabling a significant new formation or transformation of major personality elements'.

Benign and malignant matrices

The idea of a group matrix provides a powerful image for the holding and transforming power of the group. This rather deep and perhaps esoteric idea also correlates with Yalom's finding that the cohesive group is an effective group. A tightly woven net catches more fish, a tightly woven carpet is more rich. However, the group matrix, a metaphor for 'therapeutic environment', can become the container of destructive as well as creative processes. Some images that bring this to life are as follows.

1. *The spider's web*. Here a fearsome creature sits at the middle of a matrix of his or her construction. The intention of this net is to waylay innocent creatures, so that he or she can paralyse, store and devour them. There is no reason to doubt that some

group conductors may be perceived in this way and may indeed have attitudes that make them like psychological spiders regarding their group members.

2. *The labyrinth*. The matrix has been likened to a labyrinth by Hajidaki (1989), who gave a detailed and scholarly review of the associations and connections which can be generated by contemplating the labyrinth. I can only touch on this facet of the matrix briefly but have little doubt that labyrinths are very unsafe places. One may become lost for an eternity or worse still encounter a foul beast who, again, like the spider, may imprison and devour.

3. *The fishing net*. The group matrix might also be likened to a fishing net that enables wonderful and strange entities to be hauled into the group's consciousness. From time to time, however, fishing nets will haul aboard creatures that are so strange and aggressive that they cannot be contained by the fishers, causing damage to the crew and perhaps sinking the fishing boat itself. Sometimes indeed a group does bring to awareness psychological horrors that it cannot contain and may enter long periods of stagnation or disintegration as a result.

4. *The cage*. The group matrix may for a long time provide a valuable framework for its members. Eventually, however, this framework can become a cage that, while offering support, seems not to offer freedom. Indeed, one London qualifying course applicant heard a prison door clang shut when he entered his twice-weekly group for his first session. He was looking forward with dread to at least five years of captivity.

5. *Corruption of the matrix*. Matrices, it would appear can become corrupted, distorted or damaged in various ways. The metaphors for this would be knots, tangles, disconnections, roadblocks, traffic jams, the work of moles, the use of propaganda to distort information and the presence of rats in a sewage system. To follow through this chain of association one can reach the conclusion that certain kinds of destructiveness in the matrix may result from neglect or carelessness.

DESTRUCTIVE PROCESSES IN GROUPS

The fact that group processes can be destructive to both the group and its members over long periods of time has been brought into focus over the past fifteen years. Prior to this, pointers to these phenomena were given by W. R. Bion. He reported in *Experiences in Groups* (1961) how primitive and destructive modes of functioning emerged in groups whose attempts at developing defensive or co-operative solutions to the problems of being in a taskless group were relentlessly undermined by their conductor. These destructive modes of functioning he termed 'basic assumptions'. Bion had no intention that his groups would be therapeutic, and this appears to have been the experience of most of their members. However, groups that are conducted in a more nurturing and less anxiety-provoking manner than Bion's have repeatedly proved to be able to transcend the destructive forces within them and produce good outcomes for most committed and well-motivated patients. The group-analytic technique is one such method, which, in general, group analysts confidently expect to facilitate the creative management of destructive trends in their groups. None the less a flawless technique has not been achieved.

Two important ideas have been produced by group analysts, which describe and attempt to understand destructive processes in group-analytic groups. The first, by Zinkin (1983), identifies a phenomenon that he names 'malignant mirroring'. The second, by Nitsun (1991), invokes an 'anti-group' and reviews processes whereby groups set up with therapeutic intent enter phases in which darker motivations emerge.

Malignant Mirroring

> Did he live his life again in every detail of desire, temptation and surrender during that supreme moment of complete knowledge? He cried in a whisper at some image, at some vision – he cried out twice, a cry that was no more than a breath – 'The horror! The horror!'.
>
> (Conrad, 1902)

The group-analytic therapy group has been poetically compared to a hall of mirrors (Anthony, 1957). This is emphasising the experience of group members of realising that they are not only perceiving the other members of their group, they are also seeing aspects of themselves reflected in the others. In most writings on mirroring the assumption is made that the effect of finding oneself in such a hall of mirrors is beneficial to the individual and contributes to the positive development of the group. However, Zinkin (1983) makes the point that the view of oneself gained in the 'hall of mirrors' can be experienced as intensely persecuting. Seeing one's self reflected through the group process can lead to concern, transformation and growth but it can also precipitate rage, panic, denial and flight. As Zinkin suggests, the sight of one's self in a mirror can be an alienating, rather than affirming experience. However, mirrors usually display the truth (Garland, 1983). The horror for some may not be contained in the mirroring process itself nor yet in the distortions that may be present in the image. The hated and truly dreadful experience, often repudiated with considerable violence, is almost certainly an experience of the difference between what is perceived in the mirror and the individual's expectation of what he or she will see.

> One patient in a group conducted by the author was, in effect, transfixed for much of the time (as was Narcissus) in front of a mirror he held up to his life and self. He was transfixed however, not by the beauty of what he saw, but, as was Kurtz, the mysterious anti-hero of Joseph Conrad's (1902) *The Heart of Darkness*, by 'the horror, the horror'.

The psychoanalyst and group analyst are, fundamentally, engaged in a quest for the truth, with the expectation that an uncovering of the truth will facilitate healthy growth and development in the individual and the group. Some people, however, are not ready to face the truth about themselves when it arrives and indeed may never be ready to encounter their truths. These people are likely to react catastrophically if the truth arrives too soon, too explicitly or in too large a quantity. The likelihood of a catastrophic reaction to experiencing this truth will also vary according to the mode of its delivery and the context in which it arrives. A tactless confrontation in a new group is entirely different from the slow emergence of truths in an established and caring matrix. The effect on a group of the catastrophic reaction to self-discovery through mirroring is likely to be the initiation of a destructive phase or the amplification of destructive processes already in train. One such destructive phase is vividly described by Zinkin in his article.

Awareness of these issues has important implications for the selection and composition of groups and for the timing of interventions in the group process. It also gives food for thought about those patients who suddenly leave groups, whatever the manifest reason for this. It is likely that such patients are having problems facing truths about themselves which are being exposed in the group. The more energetic the departure the more likely it is that the truth will never be faced. After all, Kurtz' confrontation with his truths was on his death bed.

The Anti-Group

Nitsun (1991) points out that the belief that the group is intrinsically creative and hence therapeutic can only be the consequence of a blinkered idealism. In his experience, particularly in a new group, and particularly if errors in selection have been made, an anti-group will develop whose apparent 'aim' is to fragment and undermine the group, thereby defeating its integrative and therapeutic potential. Emerging from Nitsun's work is the crucial point that the balance between group and anti-group is far more precarious than we would wish to believe. Indeed a feather might tip it either way. Foulkes' method is above all a 'light-handed' and subtle one so that a well-timed intervention by the conductor, gently tilting the process towards group rather than anti-group, might be likened to the placing of a feather on the scales.

A reading of Foulkes and other group-analytic writers might lead the therapist to trust too readily the group's ability to become a therapeutic instrument. Foulkes, as pointed out above, proposed that group analysis is 'analysis of the group, by the group including the conductor'. Such a statement may encourage a false sense of security in the conductor and lead to a tendency to 'fiddle while Rome burns'. A modicum of mistrust in the developing matrix may be useful for the group conductor. He or she can then nurture communication in the early phases of his or her groups. It may also be as well to become mistrustful of the older group that may become set in its ways, eagerly following some well-trodden pathways while carefully and collusively avoiding the really dangerous tracks.

INTERVENING AT PIVOTAL MOMENTS

The group therapist is choosing a profession in which he or she will inevitably intervene in the lives and processes of others at a variety of levels. The theme of this book is the activity of intervening in the ongoing process of a small group-analytic psychotherapy group. The intention of the authors is to raise the consciousness of group therapists of the way in which they intervene in groups and of the range of possible interventions and intervention styles that may be open to them whilst remaining within the 'constraints' of a 'group-analytic' approach.

The role of the group therapist is to nurture a healthy group matrix. He or she may take note of the ideas presented in this section and find useful the metaphors that enable one to get a feel of the processes that may be going on in both group and members. Healthy matrices contain unpleasant and destructive elements and properties but at times the whole structure and process of a group may be developing in a way that will damage its members. At these times there is a need for the conductor to be aware of this and to develop a strategy of intervening that might enable the group to recover. This chapter has looked at the idea of intervention, with the underlying belief that the psychotherapist is developing *skills of intervention* in the psychological processes of individuals and the *group therapist* in the more complex interpersonal processes that contribute to what are popularly known as group dynamics. For much of the time the group therapist will be facilitating a benign and creative process, promoting thereby a therapeutic environment. However, it is becoming increasingly clear that the group does not necessarily move down creative pathways and most of the group situations in this book exemplify this.

There are times it seems when a group is pivoted at a point and might after that move in a constructive or a destructive direction. The energy available to the group might be used in either way. The group situations can be viewed as representing pivotal moments in the life of a group. The art of the group analyst may be seen as being in part the creative management of the evolution and resolution of such pivotal moments. It has also been frequently said that the therapeutic group represents a microcosm of normal life. Thus the management of pivotal moments in one's life is likely to be a crucial element in the art of living, which can be, as it were, practised in the protected environment of a therapy group. A key task for the conductor is to ensure the continuity of the protective environment.

The group-analytic group and conductor work together in a search for meaning in the behaviour of the group and its members, including the conductor. At pivotal moments in a group or individual's life *meaning* becomes crucial and it is here in therapy that interpretation becomes a major ingredient. In the following chapter and also in the concluding chapter the important therapeutic tool of interpretation is further unfolded and amplified.

Chapter 12

Interpretation
Why, for whom and when

Malcolm Pines

Our playwright Sheridan has one of his characters say 'begad, I think the interpreter is the hardest to be understood of the two', a comment we should do well to keep in mind when we speak our thoughts to our patients.

In my dictionary there are four different ways of understanding the term interpretation.

1. To explain or tell meaning: to present in understandable terms.

2. To act as interpreter between speakers of different languages.

3. Artistic interpretation in performance.

4. The essential meaning of something.

All these four meanings are relevant to the psychotherapist's interpretative act, which is the insertion of him or herself through dialogue into the mental life of the Other and of his or her therapeutic group.

I shall begin with the second meaning, which is to act as interpreter between speakers of different languages, for this is clearly relevant to a therapeutic group. Our patients all speak their own personal languages of neurosis and of their unique life experiences. But, though they are all unique individuals, there are also fundamental similarities through what S. H. Foulkes (1973) called the 'Foundation Matrix'. Through the sharing of a common culture rooted in a shared language and society, the majority of the patients in one therapeutic group will be connected at their deepest levels by these common roots. And for group analysis this fact is also recognised as a powerful force for dynamic change, for, though each person may, in their neurotic uniqueness, represent some deviancy from the psychological and social norm, the group itself can represent that norm from which each one differs. In the therapeutic group the pressure for adaptation and for change is towards that norm which is powerfully influenced by the group therapist's own personal and professional culture. The therapist/conductor is a member of the psychotherapeutic community, which has its own understanding of what constitutes a healthy norm for mental and emotional life. The therapist must stand for an understanding of the dynamic forces of the mind, to be aware of how disturbed development leads to problems that become symptoms that will ultimately lead the person to seek help. The therapist's learning, attitudes and experience will inevitably influence the patterns of communication in his or her group and thus the 'group matrix', which develops over time. Each person will bring his or her own personal matrix to the therapeutic situation. Here, in a variety of ways, the members of the group will live out aspects of themselves and of their problems, through the transference or through what de Maré (1972) has called transposition: a more powerful term to describe a process of complete replication of a previous life experience in a new therapeutic setting.

EXAMPLE

A woman who grew up without a father and with a very close relationship to a dominating and somewhat paranoid mother was very distressed and angry with another female group member. This latter woman had decided to leave therapy in the process of exchanging one homosexual partner for another who lived abroad. There were strong tensions between these two women. The first patient whom I described received an interpretation by the therapist that her fear and anger with this other woman arose from her need for help to deal with a powerful woman, to receive help that had been absent in her childhood through the absence of a father and other effective male figures. She responded to this interpretation with much emotion and relief. She had relived her childhood situation in the transference and had been able to accept and to use the interpretation as a much needed strengthening of her individuality. The working through of her relationship to absent men is an ongoing process in the group to which she brings her idealisation of male strength and also her attacks on men who are seen as weak.

This example brings together two categories of interpretation: that between speakers of different languages, between the two women so that they can understand their interpersonal conflict; but also the explanation to each of their own motives and experiences so that they should have a clear understanding of their inner selves.

The group analyst who, like myself, accepts the theory and technique elaborated by S. H. Foulkes has a dual role as an interpreter. He or she is a contributor both to the individual work with a member of the group and also to the dynamics of the group as a whole. Without interpretative work with the individual the therapeutic process of a long, ongoing analytic group is not possible. The groups that I work with are either once or twice a week and are ongoing over many years, whether the members are there for training or purely as patients. The aim for all is for deepening and broadening of mental and emotional life and our theories allow us a disciplined but extensive field of activity. Theories which confine the role of the therapist to dealing entirely with the group processes or which insist that all the work has to be done in the transference to the therapist are artificial limits on that necessary freedom and have been shown not to be effective as therapy.

In psychoanalysis we have a hierarchy of speech acts such as clarification, confrontation and interpretation. The most esteemed act is that of interpretation and the very least regarded is the question. Even more looked down upon is the act of replying directly to a question from a patient. But psychoanalysis is not a face to face group situation and the engagement of the therapist – whom we call the group conductor – and his or her clientele is significantly different from work in the psychoanalytic situation. We should not allow ourselves to be dominated in group analysis by the psychoanalytic model. We can use all the psychoanalytic ways of speaking but we have also a rich repertoire of other acts which centre on the process of communication *per se*. In group analysis we assert that human beings have a great capacity to understand one another at all levels. At a deeply unconscious level, as when a person speaks of a symptom, of a difficulty in life, of mental pain or conflict, the response of the other group members can often illuminate the presenting person's unconscious processes. This illumination comes from the authentic knowledge that one person has of another, based upon deep personal involvement in the therapeutic situation. The interpretations that group members give to each other are often expressions of the knowing of the other's experience. They are attempts to establish articulate, understandable verbal communication between themselves and within themselves. As human beings we have to communicate, and in the small analytic group we have a profoundly powerful situation for this communication to unfold.

The primary task of the therapist is to facilitate the communicative capacity of the group members. He or she organises the situation and defines its boundaries of time and space; he or she contributes the holding and containing which allow powerful emotions and attitudes to be experienced in safety. These are role models for containment of anxiety and emotion, for the inner digestion of raw feelings and for the articulation of clear ideas that give meaning to the therapeutic enterprise. All these are the necessary pre-conditioning for the interpretative act – the therapist's act of freedom! By his or her interpretation he or she has a moment of freedom, of liberation from the role of container. This moment of freedom can represent a temptation to the therapist, for he or she must constantly make judgements on how much he or she should listen to and how much he or she should contain and when to speak, to act. Mostly I believe it correct to listen, to contain, to process and to digest. When to act? This is the most difficult question. The simple answer is – when you have something to contribute that is valuable and which has not yet been said.

EXAMPLE

A very dominating, articulate, powerful woman has been in a once a week group for a few months. She has here aroused much conflict, but is appreciated for the strength of her personality and for the intelligence of her comments. They have come to hear of her traumatic history, of being brought up by a psychotic mother who had been repeatedly hospitalised and of a father who had abandoned the family when she was very little. Thus she was left alone not just when her mother was removed to hospital, but also during the agonising times when the psychotic paranoid process was reappearing. In this particular session she was talking about her difficulty in accepting what others offer her, which she recognised as being linked with her need to dominate and to be the giver in a relationship. She spoke about the presents that her mother gave her in childhood. There was always something wrong about them. Eventually the therapist suggested that perhaps she had always felt that the gifts came from the psychotic part of her mother. Scarcely had these words been said when she fled the room precipitously. Some ten minutes later she returned and tried to conceal her distress behind her usual cool attitude. Much time has since been spent in understanding this moment of traumatic anxiety which was released through an individual interpretation.

My belief is that the therapist has always to earn the right to make any interpretation. Truths are always personal. There is no objective, impersonal truth given by a therapist who is pronouncing objective truth about the patient. To speak out what you believe to be true about another person's life is to engage with them in a shared encounter. Any interpretation is an intervention, an entry into the private space of the other, and it is not sufficient to say that the client has come to ask for such intervention. The therapist should act from a sensitive compassion, a wish to communicate understanding which itself is based upon a sophisticated compound of empathy and of informed understanding. We feel with and for the other and at the same time draw on all our knowledge of the human condition to give form to our understanding so that the other can listen, take in and make use of our words.

Much of my work in supervision has been to get therapists to put aside their interesting and often clever interpretation and instead begin to show the patient in a group their acceptance and their understanding of them. This is done by very simple non-verbal and unverbal gestures. As Foulkes said it is not what the therapist does but what the therapist is that is important in his or her work. I also remember Donald Winnicott's words that towards the end of his life he came to understand that in psychoanalysis it is not a clever interpretation that helps the patient, for this may be done more to help a therapist to maintain belief in his own capacities, but it is *to give back to the patient what they have brought to the therapist*. That is not to take away without giving back in such a way as the patient can accept the offer. Here we are in the realm of responsiveness, of engagement, of mirroring. These are states of intersubjectivity, of state sharing, which we now begin to see as the vital processes in which mothers and infants engage from birth onwards. These activities are the basis of dialogue, of the insertion of the new-born into the matrix of the family, the process of becoming human.

There is another way to use the term interpretation. This is the aesthetic, as in the interpretation by a performer of music, by a reader of literature and of poetry, by the viewer of a work of art. It is the personal reading of the work by the performer through subtleties of timing, of rhythm, of harmony. The act of interpretation can have that aesthetic quality. Some of that should always be there but there are times that it can be so more fully and then this is an act of creativity, an offering to an audience. And it is the response of the audience to this form of interpretation that represents a completion of the interpretation. It is the resonance of the individuals, the change of atmosphere and of mood in the group, the appreciative sounds, the reflective moments, the feelings of having been understood and nourished by the understanding that give back to the therapist in fuller form what he or she has tried to communicate to his or her patients.

Interpretation is also an act of translation. The therapist expresses in another language, one which is coherent with our understanding of human nature, a version of what the patient has expressed but also suppressed. Let us take a symptom. Foulkes had said that the symptom mumbles to itself, hoping to be overheard. This humorous statement is quite profound. The symptom is a communicative act, however far that notion may be from the consciousness of the patient. In a group the responses that it arouses in the other group members and the therapist are parts of the key to understanding the hidden code in which the patient is forced to express him- or herself. A new group has a limited range of communication, as its capacity to contain, to hold and ultimately to understand what people are expressing in their illnesses is limited. Over the time the range of responsiveness and understanding greatly widens. The group then becomes a sensitive instrument through which most profound and important responses occur.

EXAMPLE

In the same group in which the homosexual woman announces her intention to leave the group, another woman remembers when this patient first came to the group she had been hostile to her because of her homosexuality and found that she had come to accept that and to accept the other person and to explore within herself what it was she had been compelled to block out. She could see now that her own sense of deprivation of maternal care and understanding had led to a hidden envy of the warmth of the other woman's homosexual relationship and the way in which it satisfied her emotional and physical needs through the closeness to another woman. However, at the same time she shared her strong feeling that by abandoning the group in order to take up another homosexual relationship that woman was denying herself the pain of working through the sadness that she herself had to endure and which had greatly strengthened her. I believe that in French the term to interpret is linked to the idea of lending something to the other person. We lend parts of ourselves, our emotional strengths, our beliefs so these should be used by the patient and by the group to strengthen their capacity to listen to themselves and to understand their deeper experiences.

EXAMPLE

A group member seemed in many ways to have a fortunate life and to have had good opportunities for emotional development. However, other members, particularly the men, felt that there was something unauthentic about her way of being in the group. They felt that her strength was not given to the group in such a way that they could feel something of her warmth and goodness, but that the way she gave it provoked a sense of distancing and being mother that was uncomfortable and unwelcome. This felt like a mother who did not share a weakness with her children and who assumed that they were incapable of understanding and helping her. Through the sense of confusion that one man felt that he had in a relationship with this member, he could see that as a child he really knew that his mother was deeply depressed and unhappy, that this was also concealed and hence he was left in confusion. The responses of the other patients formed the interpretation that helped the woman to discover her maternal identification.

A group is a forum for exchange and the interpretations are a vital part of the exchange process, the attempt to exchange surface for depth, symptoms for meaning, isolation for communication. These are the beginnings of my attempts to answer my own questions. The why, for whom and the when of interpretation in group analysis.

Chapter 13

Conclusions

David Kennard, Jeff Roberts and David A. Winter

This chapter is written anticipating that the reader will have by now attempted at least a proportion of the exercises and at least have sampled the experienced therapists' interventions and our commentary.

The therapists who responded to the Group Situations Questionnaire have provided a rich mine of possible ways of influencing the development of a therapeutic group. They are all trained group analysts and therefore give deepest insight into the method of group-analytic psychotherapy. This is a non-directive, group-centred approach to group therapy with strong psychoanalytic foundations. None the less the material in this book is relevant for most group therapists who are determined to promote a group process which allows its members to retain autonomy and self-determination. This is in the best tradition of listening to and learning from our patients or clients (Casement, 1985).

OVERVIEW OF THE INTERVENTIONS

The situations presented in this book are not easy or straightforward for the group therapist. They are each, in varying degrees, moments when the therapist is under pressure to do something to avoid a harmful consequence – either to an individual or to the group's therapeutic effectiveness. The exception is the first situation, where it would be too early to predict any consequence of the interaction in the group. The interventions given in each chapter offer a view of what experienced therapists tend to say or do in a tight spot rather than how they might go about facilitating the group's therapeutic climate under more benign conditions.

This restricted focus nevertheless helps the reader with what tends to worry inexperienced therapists most, the 'what do I do if . . .?s'. In many cases, as demonstrated in the first three situations, the answer may be 'do nothing' or 'wait and see what happens'. Group analysts place considerable confidence in the capacity of group members to work things out for themselves and find a way forward and, providing no harm is about to befall any member of the group, are intent on trusting the group process. Of course there are situations, such as situations 4, 5 and particularly 8, where to make no response is not a practical option. Such events are fairly rare but it helps to anticipate what they might be like.

In the following paragraphs comments are first made on certain general features of the interventions and then examples of different types of intervention are discussed using the classification scheme described in Chapter 1. In other words, in relation to a given situation what kinds of intervention would aim at maintaining structure, facilitating process or interpreting content?

General style

With a few exceptions, interventions are delivered in clear, plain English, with little use of technical psychoanalytic terms like projection, splitting, transference and so on. The therapist keeps these to him or herself, although the respondents to the questionnaire have often used such terms in the notes following their interventions. Some of the exceptions are flights into metaphor and whimsy that are the hallmark of one or two of our respondents. As the notes make plain, the thinking behind this is to stimulate the group to think about things in a different way, although writers of this book indicate by their comments that they are not always sure that this works. The interventions are also generally brief. These rather obvious points are worth making because the developing therapist may believe that to do things properly requires demonstrating to the group the full depth of one's knowledge and understanding, or, worse, he or she may be so immersed in a particular theory as to be unaware of using specialised terms (jargon).

Goals

Group analysts tend to practise what could be called minimalist interventions: the least the group or an individual needs in order to overcome a current obstacle or move on to a point where the members of the group can take over once more. Often this results in waiting to see how the group members themselves will respond to a situation or making a brief intervention and continuing with it after a while only if the hoped for movement in the group does not occur. The gap between what is said and what is thought by the therapist is often considerable, although clearly the method of getting therapists' responses for this book has allowed them more time to formulate their ideas than they would usually have in a live group.

Developmental awareness

One of the most consistent features of the thinking described by our respondents is their awareness of the stage the group and its members have reached in their therapeutic journey. Interventions are timed and framed with the question in mind, 'what will help the group (or individual) at this particular point in therapy?' Considerations include the capacity of the members of the group to express their views openly and directly, to tolerate anxiety, to contain conflict and negative feelings within the group, and to take responsibility for dealing with a problem arising in relation to a particular member.

Developmental considerations are especially relevant when a group is new. Thus, in response to the first situation we find the following comments.

'At this early stage I'm trying to be gentle and encouraging but also to model a bit of directness.' (3/1 The first session – an apparent distraction)[1]

'A group needs its defences, especially at the beginning. . . .' (4/1 The first session – an apparent distraction)

'In a group new to each other I would want to be cautious yet be firm in my offering of a structuring of our own to hold that anxious feeling.' (9/1 The first session – an apparent distraction)

In the second situation a more pronounced pattern has set in and the respondents, while agreeing on the need to find a way and a time to deal with this, differ in their strategies. The issue is clearly summarised by the following respondent:

'The question is when is the time ripe to confront a defence and, if it is time, how to do so without seeming to attack the group and particularly X who is speaking. . . .' (9/2 Turn taking in the early sessions)

The strategies include waiting until an opportunity arises 'to help them start thinking', coming in with a teaching point about the 'cost of controlling spontaneity', interpreting the underlying presence of anger towards the conductor or shocking the group into 'something alive, here and now'.

The third situation, still in a fairly new group, produces a similar awareness of the group's developmental needs, again followed by a diversity of views about the best form of intervention:

'At this early stage of the group a direct question to John seems preferable to asking the group's feelings about his absence/depression.' (1/3 A potential drop-out)

'The group must be allowed to develop a capacity to look after its members. If I do the looking after I deprive the group of the possibility to develop such capacity. . . .' (30/3 A potential drop-out)

In the sixth situation the issues revolve around the stage that one member has reached in her relationship with the group. This is picked up by one respondent as follows:

'It's at these most painful points that you can gain most if you stick it out and work through it. One of my groups calls this the "pain point", it is such a critical time. . . .' (6/6 Threatened premature termination of therapy)

Another respondent feels able to rely on the group:

'In a mature group I usually take a neutral position to patients who plan to leave, leaving it to the group to confront the possible defensiveness of the move. . . .' (4/6 Threatened premature termination of therapy)

The maturity of the group is also taken into account in respondents' reactions to the seventh situation.

'The group appears cohesive; usually after the phase of idealisation the group will become more realistic. . . .' (1/7 Disillusionment with therapy)

'After 2 years a group can need and tolerate longer silences and space. . . .' (4/7 Disillusionment with therapy)

'Group is a long standing one, and I'm guessing they have the stamina to leave this one dangling till next week. My remark shows I'm still alive.' (7/7 Disillusionment with therapy)

What is interesting to see is that, although our conductors are alert to the group's stage of development as a group, their reactions may vary from actively supporting the group's developing capacities to holding off from doing this so as to allow the group to try for itself. Use is also made, at critical developmental moments, of didactic explanation of the process in the group or sometimes more confrontative or provocative statements which are intended to get the group to change track by, as it were, switching the points on the railway line.

Thus therapists who have a fairly similar understanding of where the members of a group need to get to have markedly different approaches to helping them get there.

MAIN TYPES OF INTERVENTION

Maintenance interventions

It is the experience of many therapists that their work continues most satisfactorily if it is conducted within a safe, predictable, unambiguous structure. They would see an important part of their task to be the maintenance of this structure and direct some interventions to this end when the structure appeared to be threatened. Foulkes (1975, pp. 99–106) indicated that he saw this as an important part of the conductor's task when he said that the group conductor was the 'administrator' of his or her group. Implicit in this is that the long-term fate of a group and its individual members is determined to a significant extent by the initial conditions provided by the conductor and group members and the conductor's success or otherwise in maintaining a strong frame with a clean field within. The 'clean field' will be one not contaminated by the conductor's preoccupations, neuroses, foibles, life problems, projections and prejudices. Robert Langs (1978) gives vivid examples of the therapeutic process becoming almost entirely corrupted by therapists who introduce gratuitous material of their own making into the therapeutic dialogue.

Maintenance interventions are those aimed at clarifying or reaffirming a boundary. The boundary may be of place, time, membership or task and may concern the boundaries of the group as a whole or of a particular member, including the conductor.

Examples of maintenance interventions in the preceding chapters are as follows:

> I would smile at John as he entered, possibly with a nod or gesture inviting him to sit down. At an appropriate stage I would address John: 'We had been wondering about your absence without any message. What happened?' I would restate reasons why regularity and punctuality are important (taking care not to sound like an ultimatum) AFTER he had given an answer and likely reactions from the group. (1/3 A potential drop-out)

The conductor reaffirms boundaries of time and membership: to function effectively a group needs as far as possible to have all of its members present throughout each and every session.

> 'You know that you come to this group for what we understand as "therapy". If we were meeting as friends the pies and wine would be delightful but we must understand why the group 'needs' this party and then perhaps after the group is over we may feel that it is OK to join together in food and drink.' (5/5 An invitation to a Christmas party)

The conductor clarifies the boundary separating activities which are part of its task and those which are not.

> 'I am not clear whether this is your last group or not. Somehow we need to make a decision because we all need to say goodbye if you are leaving. If you wish to stay on then the place is still available because I have not yet spoken to any prospective new member.' (5/6 Threatened premature termination of therapy)

The focus is on the boundary around membership: the group needs to know if the member in question is about to cross this boundary, as what the group will say to a fellow member is different from what they may wish to say to a departing member.

'In the group we can talk about being angry but I'm not prepared to have any physical attacking here.' (28/8 A threat of physical violence)

'As I explained to you before your joining this is a TALKING GROUP – can you try to say what you feel in words, then perhaps we will be able to get somewhere with it.' (30/8 A threat of physical violence)

The conductors here are forcefully affirming that the task of the group is to talk about feelings, and that behaviour which threatens the group's capacity to carry out this task is not acceptable.

Facilitation

The role of the group conductor may overall be seen as a facilitatory one. From this point of view the group's life, process and eventual culture are implicit in its initial conditions. As with the opening of a flower or the emergence of a butterfly from its chrysalis so will the group unfold. The conductor is present to ensure the process continues and to intervene if the group becomes stuck or sidetracked. Such interventions can occur at various levels. In the coding system presented in this book two main levels of facilitation are identified, namely 'open' and 'guided'. Open facilitation is aimed at promoting the group process without the conductor seeking to influence what direction that process will take and without making any reference or allusion to unconscious processes occurring in the group. Open facilitation is, in effect, a lubricating activity, to facilitate movement in whatever direction the group chooses to go. In some cases such interventions involve a statement about what has been happening in the group and asking members what they feel about this. Other studies of therapists' behaviour sometimes refer to this as 'clarification' or 'reflecting back'. An example would be:

[I would] let him go on – let the group respond. Towards the end of the session [I would] say, 'It seems to me that this group is falling into a pattern of one member/ one session. How do people feel about that?' (4/2 Turn taking in early sessions)

This form of intervention is relatively easy to use, as it does not depend on the conductor having a hypothesis about the underlying issues or dynamics in the group, and may give the conductor time to think. Indeed, the conductor may use such an intervention to gain the group's assistance in this task (of thinking) by saying something like, 'I wonder what everyone thinks is happening in the group at this moment.' There are not many examples of open facilitation in the selection in this book, perhaps because we did give our respondents time to think!

The second level has been called guided facilitation, which falls between open facilitation and interpretation (see below). Guided facilitation is much used by group analysts as it gives the group a nudge in a certain direction while allowing the group to do most of the work, in line with the minimalist approach referred to earlier. Here the therapist has a hypothesis about what is going on beneath the surface of the group, the underlying theme or latent content, and says enough for the group to pick this up, if the members are ready to explore it for themselves. If the group is not ready then the offered direction will not be taken up and nothing is lost. The following example is taken from the same situation as the example above and sounds rather similar:

'I have noticed over the weeks that you all seem to have silently agreed to stick to a certain pattern in the group where you equally share out the time and attention in the group. Any ideas about this?' (17/2 Turn taking in early sessions)

What makes the two interventions different is the reference to 'equally sharing out time and attention'. The second intervention invites the group to consider what might happen if time and attention were not shared out equally, facing them with the risk of competition, envy and greed emerging in the group. However, the invitation is worded so that it can be responded to with whatever degree of awareness or willingness to disclose that the members may possess at this point in the group. A slightly more explicit piece of guiding occurs in the next intervention:

'I'm beginning to wonder if people *in* the group share some of those negative attitudes to psychotherapy that we've been talking about. I've noticed that often when we talk about something outside the group it can be tied up with what people are feeling in the group – right now.' (16/3 A potential drop-out)

By adding a 'teaching' element the conductor gives the group the choice of taking up the intervention on a more personal or more general level. Guided facilitation may be regarded as the conductor providing a stepping-stone for the group, or an individual, to explore the latent meaning of the behaviour in the group. The following intervention illustrates this:

'I have a feeling that there is something which may seem familiar in your situation, and that you seem to be expecting that I might mind, or be angry with you.' (17/4 A member seeks approval for concurrent individual therapy)

This comes close to an interpretation, but the therapist notes that 'a heavy transference interpretation would be tantamount to retaliation'. This leads on to consideration of interventions which are clear interpretations of the underlying content or meaning which can be inferred from the surface interactions in the group.

Interpretation

In psychoanalysis the pre-eminent intervention is interpretation, and in the opinion of some analysts the only therapeutic intervention is a transference interpretation. This is not entirely surprising in that psychoanalysis is fundamentally an attempt to enable the patient to understand his or her unconscious better. Some translation or interpretation of the unconscious will inevitably be required for this. Moreover, psychoanalysts have gradually moved from seeing transference as an impediment to therapy to viewing it as the *sine qua non* of the psychoanalytic process. A more moderate view would be that many different interventions can move a therapeutic process forward but that some are more powerful than others. The findings of this book by and large support this view but do not, and are not intended to, give a clear indication as to what provides the most powerful therapeutic leverage. None the less David Malan's (1979) triangle of coincident circumstances most likely to lead to significant therapeutic movement points in the right direction. He suggests that the most powerful moments in therapy are when the patient and therapist experience a simultaneous relationship between: events in the patient's current life, events in the transference, and formative events or patterns of events in the patient's past. Malan was talking about individual therapy but the same may be said of group analysis.

A profound difference between the two therapeutic activities is that in individual therapy the analyst/therapist is viewed as the primary interpreter, whereas in group analysis the group process is expected to take on this role; that is, if we are to accept Foulkes' (1975) definition of group analysis as: *analysis of the group, by the group including the conductor!* The conductor's work here is seen as leaning much more towards a facilitatory role rather than a predominantly interpretative one.

As indicated above, guided facilitation can be used by a conductor to test the group's readiness to explore the hidden meaning, motive or anxiety underlying the group's behaviour. By contrast, an interpretation states as clearly as the therapist is able what he or she construes the underlying meaning to be. The risk is that when the therapist 'shoots his bolt', to the group it may sometimes seem like a 'bolt from the blue', with the therapist momentarily assuming the identity of the god Thor. The advantage of a well-considered interpretation is that it leaves the group in no doubt about the conductor's thinking as he or she spells out the underlying impulse, anxiety or wish that, in the conductor's view, is giving rise to a particular pattern of defensive behaviour within the group. The disadvantage is that interpretations can be seen as retaliatory or belittling since they clearly imply that the therapist knows something about the members that they themselves do not know, and probably do not wish to know. This is demonstrated in the following intervention in the same situation as above.

'I think that you may be acting out a childhood wish-fantasy for the whole group about having a special relationship with one parent to the exclusion of everyone else. By setting up this situation you are repeating a childhood problem rather than resolving it.' (19/4 A member seeks approval for concurrent individual therapy)

Similarly the next intervention makes explicit the underlying anxiety that is hinted at in the 'turn taking' situation.

> 'I wonder if our recent "let's talk one-at-a-time roundabout" is a way of saying that it feels dangerous to compete for a place in the group at the moment without this extra safety net.' (20/2 Turn taking in the early sessions)

Part of the art of delivering an interpretation is to avoid a 'know-all' quality that may often accompany it, by appearing to speak from the patient's side, as it were. The next intervention manages to interpret a group's unconscious wish in this way.

> 'Last week there was a lot of concern about John, wondering what was keeping him away – yet today no one seems able to say anything to him. I think perhaps everyone feels a bit helpless and really expects me to deal with it and make the group feel a bit more comfortable.' (21/3 A potential drop-out)

When should an interpretation be used? It might be suggested that this would be first and foremost when the conductor is clear in his own mind what the underlying dynamics of the situation are. If, moreover, attempts to encourage the group to make a step for themselves have failed and the conductor believes that despite this the group is sufficiently primed or charged by the events occurring within it to want or need to access the new level of meaning which they are not able to reach unaided, then an interpretation may be required.

OTHER TYPES OF INTERVENTION

The four types of intervention described above – maintenance, open facilitation, guided facilitation and interpretation – cover most of the interventions routinely made by group analysts. However, other types of intervention do occur from time to time, and of course group therapists using different models of group work use other types of intervention. In the research that preceded this book four other types of intervention were identified.

Action

Psychodrama and Gestalt therapy groups use action methods as a major form of intervention. In the present examples action was restricted to the response of some therapists to the situation posing a threat of physical violence, mainly in the interests of self-defence! In general group analysts refrain from moving around or touching the group members as a form of intervention, but there is no absolute rule about this. Some may go along with a spontaneous desire to comfort a neighbouring group member with a gentle touch, acknowledging afterwards (to themselves or a supervisor) that this was stepping out of role and discussing the consequences of this. Actions of an administrative nature, such as bringing in an extra chair if the number had been miscounted or opening a window on request, would be fairly routine.

Self-disclosure

In group analysis this usually refers to the conductor expressing his or her personal feelings about a situation in the group. Disclosure of personal information or history by the therapist has little place in group analysis although it may be more acceptable in those types of therapy groups in which the therapist explicitly uses him or herself as a role model. Disclosing one's own personal response to a situation may be particularly effective in situations where there is a lot of group resistance. The surprise thus provoked may generate unexpected reactions, leading to new thoughts or feelings emerging. Examples quoted in previous chapters include the provocative:

'It seems to be safer to stay with your personal dramas than relate to each other. It's rather boring.' (23/2 Turn taking in early sessions)

the melodramatic (slightly tongue in cheek one feels):

'Well – I feel utterly shocked inside (with a sort of comfortable detachment from the counter-transference). We've been meeting as a serious group all year, and it's just disappeared, and replaced with all this, I feel quite devastated.' (11/5 An invitation to a Christmas party)

and the wonderfully pithy:

'Yes.' (1/4 A member seeks approval for concurrent individual therapy)

Modelling

In his classic textbook on group psychotherapy, Yalom (1985) describes how one of the basic ways in which the therapist shapes the norms of the group is by assuming the role of a model-setting participant. In a way a therapist is doing this all the time whether he or she thinks about it or not. Group members, as they gain confidence in the group, will often begin, both consciously and unconsciously, to use other members of the group as role models both within the group and outside. The therapist, to the extent that he or she is idealised by members, will be a particularly important role model. What he or she says or does, particularly mannerisms and preferences, will be picked up and emulated. While relatively few interventions quoted in this book could be seen as primarily intended to offer a 'lead' to the group on how to interact with others, many of the conductor's interventions do offer a way of thinking or expressing oneself that suggest what the conductor regards as desirable. Some of the clearest examples of this are in fact the examples of self-disclosure, in which the therapist is stating by demonstration that more openness or direct expression of feeling would be a good thing. Often modelling is about breaking new ground that members have been hesitant to tread on, thus taking a lead that others may follow. Examples include 3/1 above, and the following:

> 'We all want you to stay but there seems to be a fear of asking you if you will be doing so.' (2/6 Threatened premature termination of therapy)

No immediate response

While this may be seen as no intervention, it is an important string to the therapist's bow. The developmental perspective of most group analysts, described at the start of this chapter, encourages them to adopt a 'wait and see' approach for much of the time, probably more often than appears in this book where difficult moments have been highlighted. Even so many of our respondents offer interventions such as:

> I would be silent but listen attentively and encouragingly. (4/1 The first session – an apparent distraction)

> I would not intervene – certainly I would not deny X his turn when all the others have had a turn. (6/2 Turn taking in early sessions)

> Say nothing until the end – then quietly, 'It's time'. (7/7 Disillusionment with therapy)

APPLYING THE LEARNING

The intention of this book is to be of practical use for people conducting therapy groups. There are a number of ways in which learning may be achieved using the book and the material within it. Initially and most importantly there is the opportunity to fill out your own responses to the group situations both before and after reading the book. This not only gives an exercise in responding but also makes it possible to review the way in which reading the interventions of others and the commentary has influenced you.

A second exercise, implicit in the contents of this book, is to look at the classification of conductor interventions (Chapter 1, Table 3) and attempt to classify the interventions you have made. This should give some clues to your style of conducting. Do you facilitate openly or are you an informed facilitator? Is interpretation of unconscious content a favoured activity? Are you wrestling with a compulsion to be more directive and manipulative of your group or do you prefer to sit back and let them get on with it (perhaps to the point of *laissez-faire*).

There are also a variety of ways in which the material here could be used in groups. If video or audio tapes are available for supervision or peer discussion of case material then it can be a useful exercise to review the style of intervention which the conductors are adopting.

Finally, and this is also a group exercise, it has been found possible to role play the group situations as if they occupied a full group session (one and a half hours) in half an hour. This requires the role players to play their parts with less leisure and with greater intensity than in real life but none the less enables a group conductor, with or without an audience, to be confronted with the group situation and respond in something approaching real life rather than in imagination.

CONCLUDING COMMENTS

Intervening in a group is often a courageous act. Sharing one's interventions with a wider audience, including one's peers, demands an even greater degree of courage, and we are highly indebted to the group analysts who have revealed to us their likely interventions if confronted by the situations outlined in our vignettes. They are, in effect, the co-authors of this book, and we are sure that, whether you are an experienced group psychotherapist yourself or are just setting out on this path, you will have found it instructive to compare your own interventions with theirs. If you are a neophyte in this area, we hope that this experience will allow you to approach the act of intervening, or indeed the often more daunting act of not intervening, with greater courage and confidence. You will have discovered that there is no 'correct' intervention in a particular situation, but rather, within fairly broad limits, a range of possibilities, some of which will feel more comfortable to you, and more consistent with your personal style, than will others. You will also have discovered, however, that you are not faced with the anxiety-provoking prospect of being on a completely free rein in framing your interventions, and will have found in this book a way of viewing and classifying interventions which, we hope, will provide you with guidelines in doing so. These guidelines may be of particular use if you are faced with any of those very tricky situations with which you fear that a group may occasionally confront you. We know that, if your group attempts to hold a Christmas party, or a roundabout of turn taking, or even if one of its members should threaten you (heaven forbid) with a razor blade, you will now make your intervention with a twinkle in your eye!

NOTE

1 Numbers indicate intervention/situation.

Theoretical approaches to group psychotherapy

Jeff Roberts

For readers new to the field and others requiring a quick résumé a brief guide to major theoretical approaches to group psychotherapy is offered below.

Many authors have contributed in a helpful way to these tasks in a therapy group and in so doing have given the foundations for a framework to guide the therapist in making his or her interventions. Different group analysts and group therapists will have been influenced by different models. They will have selected the author(s) to help them partly through chance circumstance and partly as a result of personality traits of their own. One chooses very often to accept that which feels *right*.

A brief résumé of some useful contributions by important group therapists follows. This is not an exhaustive collection but includes people whose ideas may particularly help in the framing of interventions.

A. WOLF and E.K. SCHWARTZ have been important practitioners of a model of the 'psychoanalytic therapy group' (Wolf and Schwartz, 1962). They do not claim to treat groups or to make use of group processes except incidentally. Their claim is to treat individuals psychoanalytically in groups.

The key concepts of this approach are identical to those of classical psychoanalysis. They are: *free association, resistance, transference, countertransference, acting out, interpretation (of resistance and of unconscious content)* and *working through*. These fundamental psychoanalytic concepts will not be enlarged upon here since they can be found described in many good texts of psychoanalysis and psychoanalytic psychotherapy. The advantages of the group method would appear to be: that it is less expensive than individual analysis; that the individuals are spectators of each other's analysis; and that there are multiple possibilities of complex transference situations developing in the group.

WILFRED BION was a pioneering observer of groups who had a talent for promoting high levels of anxiety in the members of his groups. He was thereby able to describe fundamental influences on group behaviour, which he named *basic assumptions* (Bion, 1961). According to Bion, a group will either be a work group or in the grip of one of three primitive modes of functioning, the basic assumptions. The group in a *dependency basic assumption* behaves as if it had met to depend on a 'leader'. In a *fight–flight basic assumption* the group behaves as if it had met to be led in fight or flight, by the leader, usually against some externally identified enemy. In the *pairing basic assumption* the group behaves as if it were meeting in order to pair off, and an underlying and primitive motivation here would be that the outcome of the pairing should be that it *leads to the conception and birth of a messiah to rescue the group from its predicament*. The pairing basic assumption group represents despair by the group members about any value in the group in which they are taking part.

HENRY EZRIEL was, like Bion, an important member of the staff of the Tavistock Clinic in the post-war period. He contributed to the development of a method of 'psycho-analysis of the group', which was taught to a whole generation of Tavistock Clinic students.

Ezriel (1973) proposed that in every meeting of a group it is possible to identify a *common group tension*. His method was for the conductor to work to identify three types of 'object relationship' emerging out of the common group tension. First there is the *required relationship*, a socially acceptable, safe and defensive mode of functioning. The members in this relationship will be discussing each other's problems or saying how much they will miss the group during the forthcoming break. Underlying this is the *avoided relationship*, which might include denied incestuous wishes or murderous rage about the conductor's self-indulgent need to have such a long summer break. Finally there is the *calamitous relationship*, which is the feared outcome of the avoided relationship being consciously acknowledged. The exposure of incestuous wishes would lead to dire punishment and murderous wishes could destroy the therapist and the group.

The therapist's role is to understand these object relationships for the group and the individuals and more or less formally to interpret them for the group and each member, towards the end of the session.

DOROTHY STOCK WHITAKER and *MORTON LIEBERMAN* also made a significant contribution to the group dynamics approach, that had an expectation that the group process could be formalised and taught as a collection of predictable phenomena which would become the background to a rigorous therapeutic method (Whitaker and Lieberman, 1965). Their description of group process and recommended technique shows a remarkable resemblance to that developed by Ezriel. The method is based on a systematic empirical investigation of the group process. The following are the important elements of their theory.

1. Focal conflict.
2. Restricting solution.
3. Enabling solution.
4. Group theme.
5. Group culture.

The focal conflict develops as each member contributes his or her own current pre-occupation which is, as it were, woven into whatever issues are current for the group as a whole. The result of this is the *focal conflict*: an anxiety-provoking identifiable conflict involving the group as a whole. This conflict is said to be made up of a *disturbing motive* (cf. avoided relationship) and a *reactive motive* (cf. required relationship + calamitous relationship).

Groups, like individuals, can tolerate only a certain level of tension and so efforts are made by a group 'to agree' a solution for the conflict. Such a solution will work only if it is consensually agreed on, however implicitly, by all the group members and also if it is effective in reducing anxiety. Such a solution may be *restrictive*, thereby taking a safe collusive and defensive pathway, or *enabling*, when the group is able to take risks and open issues up further, even if painful or embarrassing, thereby achieving maturation and movement rather than stasis.

The *group theme* has a rather technical meaning, referring to a series of focal conflicts, linked by a similarity in their disturbing motives. Each therapy group gradually establishes a unique *group culture*, which may be defined as consisting of 'the successful solutions which a group generates to deal with successive focal conflicts'.

IRVIN YALOM identified a collection of therapeutic factors, through an experimental approach that indicated those facets of being in a therapy group that had been experienced as helpful by its members (Yalom, 1985). The pragmatic group therapist may wish to intervene so that these therapeutic factors are optimally present in his or her group. A list of these are as follows:

1. Instillation of hope.
2. Universality.
3. Imparting of information.
4. Altruism.
5. The corrective recapitulation of the primary family group.
6. The development of socialising techniques.
7. Imitative behaviour.
8. Interpersonal learning.
9. Group cohesiveness.
10. Catharsis.
11. Existential factors.

Experiments suggest that one of the most potent predictors of good outcome amongst these factors is a high level of 'group cohesiveness'. In a highly cohesive group the members are involved with each other and have a strong interest in their own, each other's and the group's progress and process. In such a group all members become regular and assiduous attenders, rarely late and finding ways of coming to the group whatever their external circumstances. The conductor who can construct and maintain such a group is likely to be a successful therapist. He or she will have come a long way towards establishing a positive therapeutic environment in his or her group. In Chapter 11 consideration is given to factors that contribute towards the development of a benign therapeutic environment and factors that militate against this. The interventions of the conductor in managing these facets of his or her group are then discussed.

S.H. FOULKES offered (1975) a definition of group analysis as 'Analysis of the group by the group including the conductor'. This should leave little doubt in the conductor's mind that it is very important that the group should be allowed to develop itself as a therapeutic instrument. Narcissistically inspired displays of pyrotechnic interpretation are not required and will disable a group and its members.

Foulkes also said of the conductor's role that 'It would be quite impossible for him to follow each individual separately at the same time. He focuses on the total interactional field, on the matrix in which these unconscious reactions meet. His background is always, and should consciously be, the group as a whole' (Foulkes and Anthony, 1957). He went somewhat further in suggesting that the conductor observe his group with a free-floating attention that allows him or her to become aware of the 'location' of the most important issues for the group.

A major concept introduced by Foulkes (1973) was the 'group matrix'. This idea contributes to the important activity of establishing a therapeutic environment, and is discussed in more detail in Chapter 11.

PATRICK de MARÉ pointed out that a group can be thought of as consisting of 'structure, process and content' (de Maré, 1972). If he or she takes this on board the conductor will be able to decide whether he or she wishes a proposed intervention to address structure, process or content (see p. 20).

Emerging from the work of these key figures in the development of group psychotherapy, it can be proposed that the group analyst has two core tasks. These are establishing and maintaining a therapeutic environment and subsequently joining his or her group in the seeking and clarification of underlying meaning. Interventions may be directed towards either or both of these ends. The former will tend to require maintenance, the latter, facilitation and an interpretative activity. These dimensions of group analysis have been explored in Chapters 11, 12 and 13.

Bibliography

Agazarian, Y. and Peters, R. (1981) *The Visible and Invisible Group*, London: Routledge.

Anthony, E.J. (1957) 'The phenomonology of the group situation', in S.H. Foulkes, and E.J. Anthony, *Group Psychotherapy, the Psychoanalytic Approach*, Harmondsworth: Penguin Books. (New editions 1965, 1968, 1971, 1973. Reprinted London: Karnac Books, 1984.)

Balint, M. (1968) *The Basic Fault: Therapeutic Aspects of Regression*, London: Tavistock.

Bion, W.R. (1961) *Experiences in Groups*, London: Social Science Paperbacks.

Bion, W.R. (1970) *Attention and Interpretation: A Scientific Approach to Insight in Psychoanalysis and Groups*, New York: Basic Books.

Casement, P. (1985) *On Learning from the Patient*, London: Tavistock.

Conrad, J. (1902) *Heart of Darkness*, Harmondsworth: Penguin (1973).

Cox, M. and Thielgaard, A. (1987) *Mutative Metaphors in Psychotherapy: The Aeolian Mode*, London: Tavistock.

de Mare, P.B. (1972) *Perspectives in Group Psychotherapy*, London: Allen & Unwin.

DiLoreto, A.D. (1971) *Comparative Psychotherapy: An Experimental Analysis*, Chicago: Aldine Atherton.

Ezriel, H. (1973) *Psychoanalytic Group Therapy*, in L.R. Wolberg and E.K. Schwartz (eds) *Group Therapy: An Overview*, New York: Intercontinental Medical Books.

Foulkes, S.H. (1964) *Therapeutic Group Analysis*, London: Allen & Unwin.

Foulkes, S.H. (1973) 'The group as matrix of the individual's mental life', in L.R. Wolberg and E.K. Schwartz (eds) (1973) *Group Therapy: An Overview*, New York: Intercontinental Medical Books.

Foulkes, S.H. (1975) *Group-Analytic Psychotherapy*, London: Gordon & Breach. (Reprinted London: Karnac Books, 1986.)

Foulkes, S.H. and Anthony, E.J. (1957) *Group Psychotherapy: The Psychoanalytic Approach*, Harmondsworth: Penguin. (New editions 1965, 1968, 1971, 1973. Reprinted London: Karnac Books, 1984.)

Garland, C. (1983) 'Commentary on Zinkin's "Malignant mirroring" paper', *Group Analysis* 16(2): 126–9.

Hajidaki, R. (1989) 'The Matrix as Labyrinth', paper presented at the 10th International Congress of Group Psychotherapy, Amsterdam.

Kennard, D.K., Roberts, J.P. and Winter, D.W. (1990) 'What do group-analysts say in their groups? Some results from an IGA/GAS questionnaire', *Group Analysis*, 23: 173–90.

Klein, M. (1984) *Love, Guilt and Reparation*, London: Hogarth Press.

Langs, R. (1978) *The Listening Process*, New York: Jason Aronson.

Lieberman, M.A., Yalom, I.D. and Miles, M.B. (1973) *Encounter Groups: First Facts*, New York: Basic Books.

Malan, D.H. (1979) *Individual Psychotherapy and the Science of Psychodynamics*, London: Butterworth.

Neumann, E. (1954) *The Origins and History of Consciousness*, Princeton: Bollingen. (Originally published in German as *Ursprungsgeschichte des Bewusstseins* by Rascher Verlag, Zurich, 1949.)

Nichols, M.P. and Taylor, T.Y. (1975) 'Impact of therapist interventions on early sessions of group therapy', *Journal of Clinical Psychology*, 31: 726–9.

Nitsun, M. (1991) 'The anti-group: destructive forces in the group and their therapeutic potential', *Group Analysis*, 24 (1): 7–20.

Oxford English Dictionary (1971) Oxford: Oxford University Press.

Roberts, J. (1983) 'Foulkes' Concept of the matrix', *Group Analysis*, 15(2): 111–26.

Sandler, J., Dare, C. and Holder, A. (1973) *The Patient and the Analyst: The Basis of the Psychoanalytic Process*, New York: International Universities Press.

Whitaker, D.S. (1985) *Using Groups to Help People*, London: Routledge.

Whitaker, D.S. and Lieberman, M.A. (1965) *Psychotherapy Through the Group Process*, New York: Atherton Press.

Wile, D.B. (1973) 'What do trainees learn from a group therapy workshop?', *International Journal of Group Psychotherapy*, 23: 185–203.

Winnicott, D.W. (1982) *The Maturational Processes and the Facilitating Environment*, London: Hogarth Press.

Wolf, A. and Schwartz, E.K. (1962) *Psychoanalysis in Groups*, New York: Grune & Stratton.

Yalom, I.D. (1985) *Theory and Practice of Group Psychotherapy*, 3rd edition, New York: Basic Books.

Zinkin, L. (1983) 'Malignant mirroring', *Group Analysis*, 16(2): 113–26.

Name index

Subject index